Miracles happen - sometimes

Amanda

Thank you for your time

Phil Koch

Miracles happen - sometimes

Cliff Koch

iUniverse LLC
Bloomington

MIRACLES HAPPEN - SOMETIMES

iUniverse books may be ordered through booksellers or by contacting:

iUniverse LLC
1663 Liberty Drive
Bloomington, IN 47403
www.iuniverse.com
1-800-Authors (1-800-288-4677)

ISBN: 978-0-5954-7368-7 (sc)
ISBN: 978-0-5959-1646-7 (e)

Printed in the United States of America.

iUniverse rev. date: 09/25/2013

This book is dedicated to the memory of Pammy K. Without her sacrifice and desire to tell her story, this would never have been possible.

TABLE OF CONTENTS

CHAPTER 1

IN THE BEGINNING

Never has there been a more resilient generation as the Baby Boomers. From the years between 1946 through 1964 no other generation has not only seen massive technological and political advances, but may have participated in them. We were born to parents of the Depression Era teaching us work hard to get ahead as well as save for that one rainy day. We were barely in kindergarten when older family members would ask, "What do you want to be when you grow up," as well as "What colleges do you plan to go to?" That was pretty heavy stuff we were bombarded with when in fact all what we were concerned with in our little world was finger painting and playing tag at recess.

As we became older, we advanced in our education as well. Each year we were taught the fundamentals helping us to go out into the world and place our mark in society. At the same time we had a medium our parents did not have, television. Not only were we limited to programs that entertained us, we also saw a changing world before our very eyes. We saw social unrest down South while civil rights were brought to our attention. We saw political leaders cut down by assassins while four youngsters from England appear on a February night and changed our lives forever. We saw our major cities go up in flames with civil unrest while we saw an American land on the moon. All while this was going on we had nightly reports of a war half way around the world that divided our country. This wasn't exactly a rosy picture before we entered the decadent Seventies.

But we persevered! As we entered our twenties, most had their degrees, were already part of the work force and began to settle down by marrying who we believed to be our soul mates. That's where I come in. After years of fumbling around school, I finally earned my sheepskin and attempted to make an impact on the working world. With what I learned and with little street smarts I managed to enter the corporate world. I made a promise to myself to first become established with a steady income before entering matrimonial bliss. That is where my soul mate enters the picture, Pamela.

We met my second semester after I transferred to one of the state universities. Surprisingly, we had two courses together. I was in my junior year earning my psychology degree while Pam was concentrating on a double major, psychology and physical education. I always thought this was the cause of her ulcer and subsequent surgery. Years later it appeared to be a more sinister underlying cause. In spite of this, we date four years before taking the plunge.

The first six months were fantastic! We were husband and wife sharing our lives and ourselves to strengthen our bond. It wasn't until the fall of 1980 when storm clouds began to gather. Pam began to exhibit major flu like symptoms. These were the same symptoms that landed her in the hospital one week before we were to be married. While trying to stabilize her, the doctors were puzzled what was causing this. Two days prior to our wedding one of the doctors wanted to perform an endoscopy. Pam would be anesthetized while a long tube with an optic lens is inserted down the throat into the stomach. Knowing the anesthetic would wipe her out for a few days, Pam refused to have this procedure. She was in stable condition and was released that same day. Although she was weak and tired, we managed to get through our wedding day. Now, the same thing was happening again. We treated it as if she had the flu. When she started passing blood, she ended up in the hospital.

The doctors preformed all kinds of procedures, but could not come up with an answer. It wasn't until one afternoon Pam was running a high fever. The medical staff did everything to stabilize her to no avail. By that evening we knew it was something very serious judging by the concerned look on the nurse every time she took Pam's blood pressure. That night she could not sleep because the pain was overwhelming. The staff tried everything to accommodate her.

The following morning x-rays were taken of her abdominal area. What the technicians discovered the entire abdominal area was clouded over as if some type of substance was inside of her. Now we were faced with a serious situation. She needed surgery immediately, but her high fever may prove fatal. The hospital called me at home and I had to rush down there to sign the authorization for surgery not knowing if she would survive. They proceeded with the surgery while I sat in the waiting room a complete basket case.

We were very lucky with the doctor who performed the surgery. It turns out he had seen this same type of disease one other time during his surgical career. In short, Pam had blisters all throughout her intestinal tract. During one of her procedures, barium had penetrated the blisters and began to fill up her abdominal cavity. Not only did he have to clean up the mess left by the barium, but all the blisters had to be popped as well. In order for her intestinal tract to heal, a temporary colostomy was made. For those of you who don't know what a colostomy is, an incision was made on her transverse colon allowing the waste flow into a plastic pouch. She would remain like this for three months before the surgeon closed up the colostomy. She remained heavily sedated with massive doses of antibiotics being pumped through her body. This was my first test affirming my vow of in sickness and in health.

With a lot of prayers and some luck, she survived this near death experience. As a result, she had a massive weight loss that affected her rest of her life. She never did regain her weight back, which should have been a warning signal. For the next couple years she was closely monitored while she carried around her massive incision mark reminding what she had been through. It was déjà vu all over again in the summer of 1983. Pam was suffering from violent bouts of vomiting and refused to see a doctor. The surgeon who saved her life believed it had to do with her previous ulcer operation. Her stomach was not mechanically sound and some major intervention might be needed. Another doctor felt there wasn't an underlying cause and Pam was doing this to gain attention, something I never told her. This went on until all the heaving began to make her weak. Again, the same surgeon opened her up and not only did he have to removed the bottom portion of her stomach including the pyloric muscle that was held open by clips, but she also had gall stones. Needless to say, the gall bladder had to be removed.

Again, we were faced with an extended convalesce while she still appeared under weight. Stopping short of Devine intervention, I began to wonder if this all would come to an end. It remained like this for the next two or three years until odd things began to happen. This began during one of our many trips to New York City. Immediately after breakfast, Pam would exhibit signs of weakness and would stop short of passing out. We thought she was becoming diabetic and began a series of tests, at which time each one came out negative. Changes were made in her diet, but she remained the same. Slowly she took the appearance of a survivor of Auschwitz.

One night, I got home from work before Pam did. No sooner I got home the phone was ringing. It was the emergency room at West Anaheim Hospital. Pam was in an accident and she was there at the emergency room. My mind went blank in that I could not remember where we live so that the nurse could give me directions how to get there. I regained my composure and eventually obtained the directions. I got there in a matter of minutes.

Upon my arrival I found Pam in the emergency room very frightened as to what was going on. Needless to say she could not remember, let alone recall how she got there. The police were already gone, but they told the attending physician according to witnesses, Pam was driving in the right lane and slowly veered off the road and hit a tree. Her car had a small ding on the front, but Pam appeared to be semi conscious. That's when someone called the paramedics. After about one hour of observation, the doctor felt she was stabilized and was released to my care and custody. I latter found out the car was still parked at the scene. After locating it, I drove it back home. The following day we scheduled a doctor's appointment, but the doctor did not find anything wrong.

One month later the exact same thing happened. I got to the emergency room and found Pam frightened not knowing what happened. What made matters worse was nobody knew what happened to the car. We waited until the attending physician discharged her. It happened to be the same physician from a month ago and he remembered Pam. Before we left he told me he is required by law to notify the DMV should he treat any driver that passes out behind the wheel. Because this was the second time in as many months, he is compelled to notify the DMV. Pam will be faced with having her driver's license suspended.

The following day, I retraced Pam's route coming home to find the car. Needless to say I could not find it. I checked down side streets and parking lots to no avail. After a couple hours spinning my wheels and coming up empty, I decided to go to the Anaheim Police Department and report the car stolen. I figured someone there would have a better idea what happened and what happened to the car. The person behind the desk did not think this would be a good idea. Instead, she pulled the dispatch sheet from the previous evening. Sure enough we found the dispatch call and found out the vehicle was moved to the police impound yard. Lucky for us there wasn't a police hold so I was able to pay the impound fees and drive the car out of there. This time the front sustained more damage than the previous hit.

Three days later the police report was available. I obtained a copy to be sure nobody else was injured or sustained some type of property damage. I read over the loss report and saw the same thing happened. Only this time Pam went over the curb and through a parking lot, missing the parked cars, but hit a steel barricade that was situated in front of a gas meter. An icy chill went down my back because if she went through the barricade, Pam would have been vaporized. The parking lot belonged to a small office. I called to be sure nobody was injured or suffered any damage. Whoever answered was happy I called because they were very concerned about Pam because she was suffering from a seizure. I asked if they were sure and I was told after she hit the barricade and they ran out there. It appeared Pam was suffering from a seizure while behind the wheel. One of their cars did get scraped but they were more worried about Pam. I told him he will be hearing from our insurance carrier to take care of the damages. After the conversation I told Pam what happened. Of course, she could not remember and she knows she didn't suffer a seizure.

The next few weeks we went back and forth to the doctor's office. Each time blood samples would be drawn and all kinds of test were completed. Each one came out negative. One night our worst suspension came true. I barely got home from work when Pam dropped to the ground and began to move about violently. Before I could clear the area she hit a rocker and coffee table and continued her involuntary movements. It dawned on me she was having a grand mal seizure. This went on for a few minutes. She was unconscious but still breathing after wards. I called the doctor's office and was told there isn't much they could do at this time. I would have to bring her in the following day for a checkup.

This pretty much was it for the next few years. The doctors placed her on anticonvulsant medication while I kept an eye on her. Once she felt a seizure coming on, she would take her medication hoping she would not have a full-blown grand mal. Sometime we were lucky and sometimes we were not. On the times we were not, I had to rush her to the emergency room so the staff could take a blood test to see if the dosages on her medication need to be changed. It wasn't until she learned to control the seizures beginning from the onset before she was allowed to go back to work. Since her license was suspended, she learned the OCTD bus routes. She was still skinny and very frail.

This went on for at least three more years before physical changes began to appear. Wounds that would not heal and scars were popping out all over. This was during the height of the AIDS epidemic. Once the doctors found out she had a number of transfusions after her intestinal surgery, HIV tests began immediately. Lucky for us they were negative. It wasn't until one night she became very weak and I rushed her to the emergency room. After running a number of tests, it was discovered her white cell count was almost nonexistent. At the same time, the doctors discovered her eating disorder. Pam spent the next month in the hospital receiving massive transfusions to build up her white cell count. After that was completed, the doctors began the long process of locating an inpatient eating disorder clinic. At first, the review board did not want to authorize payment for this because this was a psychological problem. Eventually, her doctors convinced the board to authorize and cover her in patient treatment. This began thirty days of intense counseling and group therapy.

Pam knew I was frustrated with her destructive behavior, but wanted me by her side helping her to overcome her sickness. Heaven knows how many times I confronted her after a session in the bathroom. The only answer I got was, "I don't know." The psychiatrists and psychologists could see the frustration in me during our one on one session. One day I went ballistic in front of Pam and the psychiatrist. Pam promised me to get better if I helped her. I shot back I'm not the one who has been sticking their head down the toilet bowl heaving my guts out. I knew this stunned her and placed both of us at the crossroads of our relationship.

After some very deep soul searching on my part, I decided to ride this out with her. During one weekend visit, we spoke at length what has happened and what the both of us need to do to overcome this. She finished her in patient stay and we faithfully attended the post group therapy sessions. We appeared to be going in the right direction, but this came to a stop once Pam decided not to attend the sessions anymore. This may have been a fatal mistake in the years to come.

The next few years there wasn't much change in her health, but her eating habits were rather questionable. Gradually, she became weak living on a diet of rice cakes and alfalfa sprouts. Getting up in the morning became a major ordeal in that she barely had time to get dressed and out the door headed for work. Of course, this meant skipping breakfast altogether except for the weekends. Sometimes it would take so long for her to get out of bed it would be lunchtime. Then she would have the usual, rice cakes and alfalfa sprouts. As time went on, it became more difficult for her to get out of bed, especially on weekends. If she was lucky enough to eat something, she would immediately take a shower. By the time the shower was over, she would have to lie on the bed out of breath and sweating profusely. It would get to the point she would have to take sips of Gatorade before she would be able to stand up again. By the time this was finished it would be the middle of the afternoon. Many times I would rush her to the emergency room. After the blood tests were completed the only problem was her potassium levels were extremely low to the point she was prescribed potassium supplements to raise her levels. At times she was so weak she needed help up the stairs to the second floor where she used to work. This alarmed her co-workers, but she would vehemently refuse to go see a doctor, let alone allowing them to call the paramedics. This and a few nights of uncontrollable diarrhea would take a heavy toll allowing her to function as a human being. This led to a most incredible story of survival, loyalty and test of faith for one another.

CHAPTER 2

ONE DAY MY LIFE CHANGED DRAMATICALLY

One day my life change dramatically. In a matter of two hours I went from being an active athletic person to an extremely ill, near death individual. It's amazing how fast things can change. No one can predict the future, or its outcomes of the things God has control of.

I'm not saying that one can't change a situation, but there are options to help get through such times. The week before Christmas, 2002, I came down with a severe acute case of pancreatitis. I had no idea of the severity of the disease, nor the residual effects. I was busy planning Christmas dinner, shopping and baking. I did not have time to get sick. The morning of December 21, 2002, I could not stand the pain in my stomach and couldn't take a few steps without having to lie down and rest while gasping for air. I had sent my husband, Cliff, out grocery shopping while I did a few chores around the house. Imagine, two hours changing sheets on the bed. I had zero energy. Our Boston terrier, Onslow, just looked at me with a furrowed brow sensing I was ill. I told him that I'm sick and thought I was going to die. The dog would not take his eyes off me.

Cliff came home finding me white as a ghost having difficult time breathing. He quickly called the hospital. The emergency nurse advised him to either call 911 or go directly to the emergency room. I couldn't walk down the stairs to the car, so Cliff carried me down to the car. There, I just curled up in the back seat. Once at the hospital, staff members brought a wheelchair out to the car and rushed me to the E.R. I was in so much pain plus I had the chills. The doctor came in, asked a few questions, ordered some lab tests and set up an I.V. solution. He also ordered morphine and an anti-spasmodic for my stomach. The pain was so bad I ended up receiving four shots of morphine and three shots of the anti-spasmodic medication. Later on, the doctor suspected pancreatis. A series of x-rays and an ultra sound confirmed his diagnosis. He told me I would need to spend a few days in the hospital. I was admitted to a private room on the fifth floor. I figured I would be there for a short time, but little did I know what I was up against.

I actually started having the symptoms during the summer and saw my doctor a few times. They ran the usual blood work telling me my potassium levels were low and prescribed pills. I was still huffing and puffing while walking short distances. While at work, I had to be helped up the stairs and across the office to my desk. I kept on going back to the doctor, but she could never figure out the problem or what was wrong other than my potassium levels.

During the first few days, I was under the impression I would be fine after some medication. For a short time I had nothing to eat except for the clear liquid diet the doctors ordered. My sister, Eileen, spruced up my room with Christmas decorations and gave me socks to keep my feet warm. I also remember carolers coming in my room on Christmas Eve. I began to cry because I was missing being in church for Midnight Mass. I remember spending Christmas day with my husband, mom and dad. The following days, neighbors and friends came to see me. Later, I thought I saw the New Year come in, but according to my husband I was already unconscious in I.C.U. I remember waking up in a different room then my original room I was in. The nurses were saying something about me trying to pull out all my tubes and get out of bed.

The next time I woke up was in March 2003. My left hand was heavily bandaged and I could not speak due to the fact I was on the ventilator. I couldn't even move because I was so weak. My parents and husband were with me every day. I still did not understand the severity of my situation. I had a team of specialists, one for every organ and system in my body: lung doctors, kidney doctors, vascular surgeons and an infectious diseases specialist. I started a daily routine of kidney dialysis that eventually went down to three times a week.

In the beginning, dialysis was so difficult for me. I was anxious and getting panic attacks during the treatment, which took between three to four hours. Thank God, now I was down to two and one-half hours. I used to take anti-anxiety medicine and pain pills. Sometimes, I would either watch a movie or listen to CD's. I had regular dialysis nurses while in I.C.U., but after I was transferred to a rehab hospital, I had a different nurse each time. Everyone was very nice and did special things for me. Teri used to bring something from Starbucks. She even gave me a small hand-held electronic game. Helen would sometimes bring me a latte or small gifts, such as hair accessories, bracelets and even a rosary. Denver brought me Belgian chocolates. Last, but not least, Steve would burn copies of various CD's and even gave me a laptop.

According to my husband, Cliff, I was in a coma. During this time, I went for CT scans to see if there was any brain activity. As long as there was brain activity, Cliff saw to it I was kept alive. After I was out of the coma, I became acquainted with all the staff in I.C.U., the doctors, lab and x-ray, kitchen and housekeeping. Everyone in the hospital knew me. Dad would drop off Mom everyday on his way to work and would come by afterwards for a visit. Cliff would visit after work, on weekends and sometimes if he got the day off.

I was dying to go outdoors. After all, it had been since December that I was in bed. In April, my doctors took me on a small outing. A respiratory therapist with an oxygen tank, the lift team, my nurse for the day plus a couple doctors pushed my bed through the halls down to the service elevator. We all went outside to the courtyard to soak up some sunshine. It was a beautiful day! One month later, the team of us did it again. It was like a portable I.C.U for the outdoors.

CHAPTER 3

BY THE END OF MAY

By the end of May, I was ready to be moved to a rehab hospital or skilled nursing facility or simply known as a nursing home. Whatever one calls it, they are all the same even though some pride themselves on the rehabilitation aspect of the facility. I remember arguing with the nurses that I did not want to go anywhere but home. I did not want to go to a nursing home; I wanted to go home! Well, I didn't win that battle. I ended up at New Orange Hills Rehab Hospital in Orange, California. My first impression of the place was of mixed reviews. I was placed in a triple bed room with a comatose lady and a feisty one who died after a couple months. During the first two days, the staff was doing evaluations on me: physical and occupational therapy, dietary, various doctors and nurses saw me. Respiratory therapists gave me breathing treatments and continued to work on weaning me off the ventilator.

After the first few days of paperwork and evaluations, I was getting used to the daily routine. I woke up at 7:00 A.M. for breakfast, waited for my nurse's aide to bathe me then got me ready for the daily activities, physical and occupational therapies. Before long, I knew everyone in the facility. In activities, everyday something was planned. I went to cooking classes, arts and crafts, music sing along and movie matinees. My favorites were arts and crafts and cooking. I painted little jewelry boxes, picture frames, made beaded bracelets and earrings, sewed hand puppets and made various holiday decorations for each specific month. It was fun. In cooking, we made lots of soups and stews, some tasty and others not.

My physical therapy was nicely coming along. I still had my feet, petrified with gangrene, but I was able to walk on my heels and ride the stationary bicycle. I also was using weights and doing leg extensions for my quadriceps and curls for my hamstrings. As I was getting stronger, my vascular surgeon, Dr. Sidney Glazier, started talking about the amputation of my feet and ankles. We made a few office visits to discuss the procedure. Also, while in his office, he amputated two of the fingertips on my right hand. The tips were dead with gangrene. I sat and watched as he injected the local anesthetics, took the scalpel and cut off the tips. Cliff was with me and watched the entire procedure. We set the date of July 22, 2003 for the amputations. According to Cliff, I'd be walking like Lt. Dan from "Forest Gump".

I met all kinds of friends, staff members and patients at the rehab hospital. We would eat together in the dining room, laugh and have a good time as can be expected with all our problems. Everyone had some sort of difficulty, but all tried to make the best of it.

It came time for my scheduled surgery. I was picked up by the ambulance company sometime around 7:00 A.M. taken to Kaiser Permanente Hospital in Anaheim for surgery to begin at 10:00 A.M. As is always in the case, there was a delay. All I could dwell on was the fact that I was hungry and was not allowed any food or drink until after the surgery. I don't remember what time I finally got to the operating room, but when I woke up I was taken to I.C.U. and it was around 10:00 P.M. Wow, what a long day! As the pain was setting in, I asked for my pain medication. I was given a morphine pump so I could self-administer the medication. I remained in the hospital for three weeks. I stayed with my mom and dad until my husband could get his family medical leave. I stayed at my parent's home for four days until I had a relapse and was taken by paramedics to Whittier Hospital. Once I was stabilized I was transferred back to Kaiser in Anaheim. I still had the bandages from the amputations along with six inch pins coming out from where my feet used to be. This was so I could not put any weight on them. I learned how to transfer from a chair, to the couch and the commode quite fast. Slowly but surely, I was getting used to my new lifestyle.

After spending some time in the hospital, I was discharged to my own home where my little Boston terrier was so excited to see me. He would not leave my side. Cliff had to carry me from room to room since the wheelchair did not fit through the halls. I spent a total of two days at home before developing a severe infection and was rushed back to I.C.U. for almost two months. I could not stay out of the hospital for any given length of time. Each time the doctors were about to write me off, but I showed them. With my faith and trust in the Lord, there was nothing going to stop me. Every day, all day I would pray to the Lord Jesus to heal me, give me strength and courage to make it through another day. I truly believe that my faith was an integral part of my recovery. Without it, most likely I would have died.

CHAPTER 4

FINALLY, I WAS DISCHARGED

Finally, I was discharged from the hospital. I went back to my parent's home again. Boy, which was an experience in itself. I was still bandaged from the amputations and confined to a wheelchair. I learned to transfer from chair to my bed and also the bedside commode with use of a slid board. It's a little board used to bridge the gap from the wheelchair to the sofa, commode or any other surface. I just shimmied across the board to the new location. I got pretty good at the transfer board in a matter of a couple days. It was kind of nice back at my parent's home, but not for a permanent location. I visited with Mom during the day as she helped a great deal with my care. She bathed me and washed my hair. She would make my lunch and snacks. It gave her a sense of responsibility taking care of me now that grandmommy had passed away.

Dad was busy working, so it was mostly Mom and I together. We learned by trial and error maneuvering the wheelchair through the home and adjusting to my new way of lifestyle. My legs were still bandaged from the amputations and I was told not to put any pressure on them. After six weeks the pins would come out and I could consider getting fitted for prosthetics.

My stay at my parent's was cut short. One day when the home health nurse came to visit, I passed out. I don't remember anything of that day. The next thing I knew I was back in I.C.U. I was taken by ambulance to Whittier Hospital where an east-Indian doctor knew my pulmonary doctor, Khalil Sivgie. Dr. Sivgie wanted me transferred back to Kaiser

Lakeview with an M.D. in the ambulance with me. I remember waking up in I.C. U. back on the ventilator.

I remained intubated for about two days and eventually back on oxygen via a nasal canula. I remained in I.C.U. for two weeks and was sent back to New Orange Hills for five days. This was supposed to regain my strength and confidence. In the meantime, Cliff was going round and round with the business office because they were demanding payment that Social Services was supposed to take care of. When Cliff came to the nursing home that night, the staff wanted to discharge me right then and there. He still did not have the authorization for his family medical leave yet, so there was no one to care for me at home. The administrators at New Orange Hills wanted me out now! So Cliff put me in the car and we went to our own home. Boy, was he furious!

We got to our home in Anaheim where my neighbors and dog, Onslow, greeted me. Everybody was so happy to see me. Cliff helped me on to the sofa and Onslow quickly cuddled up beside me. In fact, he would not leave my side. I spent the night on the couch while Onslow snuggled right in and would not budge.

For the next two days, Cliff was my nurse carrying me from the living room to the bathroom since the wheelchair would not fit. He would also carry me to the dining room. Our condo was not big enough to accommodate the wheelchair. I stayed there for a total of two days before getting a very serious infection. The Anaheim paramedics took me to Anaheim Memorial Hospital. Again, I was intubated, received a dialysis session and was placed in I.C.U. Two days later, I was transferred to my old room at Kaiser Lakeview I.C.U. There, I remained until November. Again, it became time to move me back to rehab. New Orange Hills gave a song and dance routine about not wanting me there for no specific reason. Then someone said it was an altercation Cliff had with the staff. Then they tell us they have the right to refuse service to whomever they wish. So, we had to find a facility that would take me on the ventilator and able to perform bedside dialysis. As it turned out, the only place that would accommodate me was out in Colton called Reche Canyon. I put up a big fuss not wanting to go there, but I was eventually transferred there.

The facility was much fancier than New Orange Hills, but there wasn't much in activities. They did have an in-house movie channel, hooked up to a DVD player, where I got caught up on lots of movies. I met the entire staff. Most of the CNA's must have been on some type of community service. I've never seen so many tattoos on so many people in one given place! In fact, some wore lanyards with toll free numbers for bail bonds places. I stayed there for two months before I developed bleeding from my lungs into the trach. I was transferred to I.C.U. at Kaiser in Riverside where I spent the next three months. My doctors there didn't have much hope in my recovery and were asking me if I was afraid to die.

By February of 2004, I went back to Reche Canyon. Two months later, I developed another infection and wound up back at Kaiser in Riverside. After some meetings with the staff, I was allowed to be transferred to Kaiser Lakeview since that is where my doctors are and they all know my case. My family was glad to see me go back to Anaheim. I was back in my old room in I.C.U. where everyone knew me. They were beginning to be my new family. It wasn't my favorite choice for relatives, but such is life. I stayed in the unit until May, 2004, when I was finally re-accepted at New Orange Hills. This was after a meeting Cliff had with the staff at which time he was told to be on his best behavior. All this because of Cliff 's so called "altercation", which was just a heated telephone conversation.

CHAPTER 5

I MEET SOME WONDERFUL PEOPLE

I met some wonderful people during my stays at both rehab centers and the hospitals. The majority of the nurses were so loving and caring toward me. I received so many gifts from staff members and visitors. Each time I would receive a new stuffed animal, I would name it. It got to the point I almost started running out of names. One nurse in particular, Minnie, was most caring. She would come and sing to me and pray with me. She worked on the fourth floor, but came up to the I.C.U. just to sing me to sleep. At Christmas, Minnie gave me a carved crystal egg. It revolved on a lighted base. I received numerous teddy bears, various animals, books and C.D.'s. I spent Christmas, my birthday and all other holidays, as well as my twenty-fifth wedding anniversary in the hospital. For a while, I lost all track of time.

My family was so supportive; they would visit daily. Dad would drop off Mom in the morning on his way to work and come by around 4:00 P.M. after work and visit.

CHAPTER 6

BEGINNING
OF THE NIGHTMARE

You have just completed a firsthand account of Pam's first two years of her incredible journey of surviving the residual effects of acute pancreatitis. There are many reasons for causing this, but what it boils down to is the pancreas becomes inflamed causing a severe debilitating pain in the upper abdominal area. Not only did this happen in her case, but the gastric juices produced by the pancreas go unchecked causing the body to destroy itself. In a matter of days, Pam came down with A.R.D.S. (adult respiratory distress syndrome), peripheral vascular disease, kidney failure and bilateral pneumothoraces (collapsing of both lungs). Pam was attempting to write about her experience when one of her many infections took over her body. She did not survive. The purpose of this is to finish her story and describe what actually happened behind the scenes and during the times she was either in a coma or in a state of unconsciousness.

As a personal note, those of you who suffer from anorexia and bulimia or those of you who have loved ones or friends that suffer from this, please take the time to read this. Those who suffer from this may be able to function in everyday life and go as far as denying the seriousness of what is being done to the body. Once the damage has been done, there is no turning back. I should know because I saw it firsthand.

That Saturday morning, she woke up feeling weak with aches and pain. We thought it was the onset of the flu meaning she would be sick possibly through Christmas. She asked me to go ahead and do some grocery shopping for the upcoming holiday. I was gone for about two hours. When I returned, Pam was lying on the sofa in a fetal position with her face being ashen white. I told her to see a doctor because she may have something more serious than the flu. Those who are familiar with Pam are quite aware she refuses to be fussed over if something is wrong. There were times I had to physically drag her down to the emergency room for some reason or another. A majority of the time, we were lucky and the doctors were able to help her after a lengthy hospital stay. This time, she could only shake her head no while rocking back and forth because of the pain.

That was enough for me. I immediately called the hospital describing what was going on. The nurse on the other end told me to either call 911 or go directly to the emergency room. With that, I carried her down the stairs that lead to the garage and placed her in the back seat of our 1989 Toyota Celica. While a light mist was falling, I drove off to the hospital.

Anybody familiar with the Southern California freeway system knows that regardless of the day or time of day there will be a traffic jam. As luck would have it, this is what happened as we entered the eastbound 91 Freeway. I thought of taking the side streets, but this was the Saturday before Christmas and all the roads were packed with Christmas shoppers. By weaving in and out of the traffic flow, I was able to get to the hospital in a reasonable amount of time. I pulled up to the emergency entrance and ran in asking the desk clerk to have the orderlies bring a wheelchair because Pam was unable to stand. Quickly they came out and whisked her to the emergency room. I had to stay at the front desk to give the vital information while the doctor on duty administered to her. This was approximately 2:00 P.M. After I was finished, I was allowed to go back to the cubicle she was in. The doctor had already ordered I.V. solutions and morphine for the pain. In all, she had a total of four morphine injections that had a minimal effect on her. After pressing and listening to her abdominal area, he suspected acute pancreatitis. We would not know for sure until after the x-rays, lab test and an ultra sound. I didn't say much, but while sitting on a stool, I was thinking to myself this is going to be something serious.

Pam was having problems the previous summer and had to be rushed to the doctor's office. She was constantly weak while huffing and puffing to get around. Her blood tests indicated the potassium levels were low and was given supplements to bring them back to normal levels. She also exhibited cold hands while on occasions they were turning blue. One week before this happened, she saw her doctor. Being somewhat concerned, her attending physician recommended to see a rheumatologist. Little did we know how much this would affect her well being.

Once the results were in, the attending physician was right and immediately told us she will need to be checked in for a few days. She was looking at a daily regime of antibiotics to control her symptoms. She then was moved up to the fifth floor and went through the normal check in routine. By this time, it must have been 9:00 P.M. I told her not to worry in that she will be spending Christmas in the hospital, but eventually she will be getting better. Once I got home I immediately called her parents.

The following morning, I called Pam's best friend, Joanne Compton. Both Pam and Joanne have known each other since high school. Even after Joanne joined the Air Force, both kept in contact with one another. Joanne was based out of West Germany most of the time and just outside London. She would always send all kinds of knick knacks that one would find over there. When she transferred to just outside London, there was a major pipeline from there back to wherever we were living at the time. You name it, every dress, hat and accessory from "Laura Ashley" was sent to Pam. I did not know the full extent of this until I had to go through Pam's closets. At one time, we had a chance to hook up with one another while we were visiting London. We went out with her current boyfriend, who eventually became her husband, Eddie. Joanne was quite aware of Pam's problems and requested I keep her posted on her condition.

At this time, I was still on vacation. I would get there just as visiting hours began, visit for a while, go to lunch, and visit for a few more hours and then go back home. We have a Boston terrier named Onslow after the character on the Britcom "Keeping Up Appearances". I would walk him before I left for the hospital and after I got back. He really missed Pam, but this became more evident as time went on. During this time, Pam's younger sister, Eileen, brought in Christmas decorations to spruce up her room. We tried to keep her spirits up in spite of the circumstances. At the same time, other family members and friends would come to visit, as well.

Christmas Day was fairly low key. Pam had already had our decorations out and our artificial tree was already up. It wasn't surprising that I was not in the mood to open any of the wrapped gifts. The packages were in the same condition stored in the corner where the tree would be. Eventually, they were stored in the garage where they remain to this very day. I spent a majority of the day with Pam in spite of her weak condition.

Pam's condition did not change up through Christmas. She was fairly weak from the morphine and antibiotics, but she was quite alert. Shortly afterwards, she developed a cough to the point was coughing up large quantities of phlegm. The cough gradually got worse to the point that if I knew better, I would say she had pneumonia. The nursing staff did not seem to be alarmed by this. Just before New Year's Eve, she was on an oxygen mask.

The day before New Year's Eve did not start off exciting. When I got to her room, the bed was made and nobody was in there. I ran to the nurse's station asking what is going on. The first nurse was not of any help because she was not familiar with Pam's case. Eventually, the nurse assigned to Pam that day came by saying she was moved to I.C.U.

"When did this happen," I asked.

"Earlier this morning," the nurse indicated.

"Why didn't anybody notify me," I screamed. After reading over the paper- work she indicated "we spoke to a family member this morning."

"I'm her husband and nobody spoke to me," I said frantically.

I asked if I could use a phone. I immediately called Pam's parents. I asked if they received a call from the hospital earlier today. Pam's mother, Doris, indicated they had not received a call. I told her Pam had been moved to I.C.U. and I'm about to go up there. I was given directions to I.C.U. and how to obtain permission to enter her room. Once I got there she was still on the oxygen mask and very incoherent. I figured she had full blown pneumonia and it was starting to affect her. The doctor on duty came by telling me that she was moved as a precaution in order to monitor her condition. This was the beginning of a five month stay in I.C.U.

New Year's Eve was pretty much the same. Pam was slipping in and out of consciousness while her cough got worse. By this time, I was introduced to Dr. Paul Chan, who would be one of her pulmonary doctors. He went on to say if her breathing did not get any better, it is possible they may have to place her on a ventilator to help her breath more easily. By this time I had a feeling life as we know it will never be the same.

The following day there wasn't any change. By late afternoon, not only was I there, but both her parents and my sister-in-law, Eileen, as well. Dr. Chang wanted to have a conference with us. In short, her breathing was labored and they will need to place her on a ventilator. Although Pam was semiconscious it was evident she was not aware what was happening around her. We decided to get a bite to eat while the nurses, technicians and doctors placed her on the ventilator. Once we returned, she was sedated and breathing more easily with the help of the machine. In passing, Dr. Chan did indicate this is a last resort in order to keep the breathing passages clear.

The following day, Pam was moved to room 703 in the unit. She would be closer to the nurse's station if something happened. When I arrived, I noticed both her arms were tied to the rails of the bed. I was told Pam had become very agitated and tried to pull out the I.V. and the tube that went down her throat connecting her to the ventilator. Pam was placed on a medically induced coma where she would remain for the next five months. I could only watch the ventilator keeping her alive and the monitors flashing out numbers that indicated whether or not she was in stable condition. I stood there stunned not knowing whether or not Pam would live to see another day. It was as if life came to a complete stop and I did not have any control over the circumstances. Little did I know what was to happen in the next few days would challenge the strongest physically and psychologically.

Pam's physical condition began to take a turn for the worse. Both her hands and feet became more discolored. The doctors felt she was coming down with vasculitis. Within a few days, the fingers on her left hand and partially on her right hand turned black. I worked feverishly to remove her wedding and anniversary rings before the staff had to cut them off. In the process, I took off a chunk of her knuckle, but that would be the least of her worries. The same was happening to both her feet. At the same time, her body became bloated to the point her eyes had to be covered.

By this time, I was already back to work. I told my immediate supervisor the situation. What I had to do was come in earlier and skip lunch altogether so that I could leave early to the hospital. The hospital was on the away to and from work, so that did not present a problem. I would get there between 1:30 P.M. and 2:00 P.M. just in time for one of the doctors to advise me of her status. Her mother was already dropped off in the in the morning and by Pam's bed side by the time I got there. During the morning hours, I would call the nurse's station and speak to her nurse for that particular day. Each time, there was no change in her status.

Three days later, I received some shocking news. Pam's right lung had collapsed and was in very serious condition. I told my supervisor I had no idea if and when I would be coming back and immediately left for the hospital. Once I got there, her appearance had not changed much, but her breathing was very labored even on the vent. Shortly afterwards, Eileen came by. She found out while at work and left immediately as well. The only thing we could do was to hug each other while she said "I don't want to lose her." We just stared at her hooked up to the monitors and ventilator wondering if this is it.

Shortly afterwards, the attending physician in I.C.U. pulled me to the side and went over the situation. He started out by saying Pam is very, very sick. She currently has A.R.D.S. (adult respiratory distress syndrome). Basically, this is a severe case of pneumonia, but what happens is portions of the lungs had hardened and become destroyed forever. Surgical removal would correct this, but with the collapsed lung, surgery was not an option. They can only keep her stable. Also, her case of vasculitis is guarded. Should this spread to her heart, lungs or head this could be fatal. At the same time, it is possible she is suffering from kidney failure. The doctor looked me straight in the eye saying he did not expect her to make it through the night.

I sat there frozen in space and time. I could not move, I could not blink and I could not say anything. Again, the doctor looked me straight in the eye saying "It looks like you are going to cry." I choked out the words "I don't know what I'm going to do."

The doctor went on to say they have to cut an incision in her side and insert a tube. This will clear out the air, mucus and whatever else that is trapped in the plural cavity as a result of the collapsed lung.

The doctor was called away and at the same time Marcie Crutchley, one of the social workers at the hospital happened to walk by. Seeing that I was sitting there looking like a zombie, she asked me my name. Unknown to me, Marcie was involved in Pam's case and was very familiar what has gone on since she was admitted. Once she found out who I was, she led me to one of the conference rooms in the unit. There, I poured out my soul on not only what has occurred the past few days, but I gave her a brief summary of Pam's medical history. At one point, I did not know who was in more shock, Marcie or myself. She gave me her business cards indicating if I needed anything just give her a call. This came in handy because at the time Pam became sick, she was on unemployment. Every time the check came in there was a questionnaire asking if she was able to go out on an interview. Because I checked off the box indicating no, this set off a red flag for the state and they wanted to set up a phone conference. I was having a hell of a time trying to explain she was unable to because she was in a coma. This made the state to arrange a face to face meeting to discuss this matter. Marcie was able to contact the right person explaining this was not going to happen.

By this time everybody in the family was there. Eileen's husband, Rich stayed home with their two sons. I signed the consent for the procedure and we stayed in the waiting room until it was completed. They had the surgeon complete the procedure in the room. She later came out saying everything went fine. She will be monitored and we will be notified if anything comes up. Once I got home, it was the first of three times I stayed up all night waiting for the phone to ring and began to come up with ideas for a funeral.

I dozed off maybe for a couple hours before I went back to the hospital. She was stable for her condition, but her extremities became darker in color. Shortly afterwards, her mother came up to the room. Every time she was there, Doris had this upbeat optimistic outlook saying everything will be fine and we would be celebrating a late Christmas this year. Both of Pam's parents emigrated from the Middle East to start a family here in the States. I used to tell everybody if they stayed two more weeks before coming here, Pam would have been born in Beirut. Although they were able to assimilate into the mainstream, they did retain some of the old country values, one of which was being optimistic in the face of failure or every cloud had a silver lining. I did not know how to tell them in spite of hoping for the best, the odds are not in Pam's favor. Later in the day when Eileen came by, I pulled her off to the side. She agreed with me that for a lack of a better description, her parents were clueless. We waited until her father, Lucien, came by after getting off work. We decided to discuss with them the situation before we had a status meeting with the doctors. We went on to explain this is far more serious and the chances are she may not survive. Both Eileen and I were not sure whether or not her parents understood this. A few minutes later we were meeting with two of her doctors, Dr. Chan and Dr. Sivjee. Dr. Chan went on to say Pam is gravely ill and they are doing everything possible to keep her stable. He attempted to explain in layman's terms what has occurred and what they plan to do. Both Eileen and I understood, but I was not sure if my in-laws understood. Finally my father-in-law, Lucien, asked, "On a scale of one hundred that she will live to one she will die what number is she at?" Dr. Sivjee thought about it for awhile and said, ".75." Everybody in the room sat there unable to move or say anything. Doris then asked, "Will she survive?" Dr. Chan thought about it for awhile and said something to the effect, "I have seen patients survive serious conditions." I think this was a polite way for him to say no or I don't know.

The doctors went on to say because of the clotting problem that is restricting the blood flow to her hands and feet, it is possible she could suffer a stroke without us knowing it until they perform a CT scan. There, I made the second most important decision in my life for them to constantly perform a CT scan. If it shows signs of life then we will keep her alive. The doctors warned me should she come out of the coma, there might be a possibility of brain damage. I'll take that chance if it should come up.

The following day both her parents were already there when I entered the room. Also there was their parish priest, Fr. Andrew. I was not sure but he was going through the same motions I saw when Pam's grandfather suffered an aneurysm. In other words, she was receiving last rights. I tried to keep my composure as much as I could.

The next few weeks there weren't any major changes. It was decided that they would perform dialysis to control her bloating. The first session did not produce any significant changes. The following day after being dialyzed, she passed 2,000 ml of urine. Both the doctors and nurses were encouraged about this. Since then she received dialysis three times a week. Another procedure started was platelet pherisis. As mentioned earlier, one of the complications of pancreatitis is the immune system will destroy vital parts and systems within the body. In Pam's cased, the platelets were destroyed to the point they stuck to one another causing the clotting and eventually destroying both feet and her left hand. What the platelet pherisis did was to filter out the damaged platelets and replace them with fresh ones. This was a long drawn out process and usually did not show signs if it was working until after fourteen sessions. We started to notice changes after the twelfth session. The contents returned to the containers are clearer.

I noticed her feet were peeling in that the dark areas of skin was popping up and curling. She was still in a coma so I know I could not hurt her. Slowly, I began to peel the skin that was popping up. This made her mother upset because we knew she was on blood thinners and any open wound may cause uncontrolled bleeding. Each time I peeled off a piece of skin there wasn't any bleeding, but I noticed the skin was pink underneath. I'm not a doctor, but this told me there was blood flowing in that area. Over the next few weeks I continued this over my mother-in-law's objections. Before she had her bilateral amputation, I had skin peeled exposing half her feet including both heels.

While all of this was happening, life must go on. I would still go to work early in the morning and spend the afternoons by her bedside although she was in a coma. It has been said if a person is in a coma and if the family talks to the person as well as soft music in the background the chances are greater for recovery. My brother-in-law, Rich, went out and purchased a portable AM/FM CD player. We rounded up CD's that were either soft music of classical and had that player going twenty-four hours a day. I was very thankful he was constantly buying batteries to keep it running. Every morning, Rich would stop by to see how Pam was doing. The hospital was built along the Santa Ana River. There was a bike/running trail along the banks. After Rich would finish his workout, he would stop in. Sometimes both Rich and Eileen would bring along their two sons, Grant and Chase. One would take the kids to a nearby park while the other would visit Pam. After a while, they would switch places.

As mentioned earlier, Pam was receiving unemployment when she became sick. By the time her January check came in, she was already in a coma. I could not deposit it in our joint checking account because my name was not on the check. However, we did have two separate checking accounts. After we were married I had Pam open an account solely in her name. If anything happened to me, she at least has the separate account to keep the money flowing. I checked with the unemployment to see if I would be able to at least deposit the checks and eventually issue a check payable to me to deposit in our joint account. I was told as long as I have a general power of attorney I should be able to do this. I went down to her credit union and attempted this. I was told unless I present court documentation showing I was her conservator, they could not help me. I pointed out this could takes months and get quite expensive before I could present them with the proper court documentation. The teller just repeated herself stating unless I present the court documentation the credit union is unable to accommodate me.

Needless to say, the bills were coming in. There were also a few surprises I was not aware of. The major one was her credit cards. We had an agreement we would have our own credit cards solely in our own names. We could purchase whatever and pay the monthly bill accordingly. I did not have the slightest idea where she kept her incoming bills. I also found out the hard way that two bills were due just as she went into the hospital and at the beginning of the month. The name of the creditor will remain anonymous in order to protect the innocent and prevent any frivolous law suits. One night I received a call from this one particular creditor wanting to know why Pam did not make her monthly payment. I explained to him the fact that she was in a coma and we don't know what the outcome will be. It was as if the idiot was reading from a script and telling me something to the effect they are sorry for my situation, but unless I send a payment overnight with the late fees included, I will jeopardize Pam's credit. With the utmost restraint, I calmly repeated myself saying she was in a coma and the outcome is uncertain. Again, he repeated his little speech he was instructed to deliver if I did not cooperate. I told him I will see what I can do and hung up.

I waited until the January statement came in. I went ahead and dipped into our savings to make the minimum payment. A couple weeks later I received a call from the same creditor. Again. They went through the same song and dance routine saying they expected two months of payments and late charges. Unless I send a payment overnight it will jeopardize Pam's credit. Again, I explained that Pam was still in a coma and the outcome is still uncertain. Unless this person was hearing impaired, they continued to repeat the same scripted speech. Again, I told them I will see what I can do. I waited for the February statement and this time I paid the two months plus the late fees. Two weeks later I received another call from the same creditor. This time they were telling me they have yet to receive the payment. I went ballistic. After a number of references of the person's family ancestry, references to biology and religion I ended the conversation by saying something to the effect for them to wait for the (expletive) payment to post and don't bother me anymore.

Unknown to me I had the kitchen window open. I heard my little tirade echo down the alley between the condo units. I don't know if anybody heard it, but I never did receive a call back from the creditor.

For the next five weeks, life as we know it did not change much. Pam was still in a coma with the ventilator doing all the breathing while the nurses kept an eye on the monitors. The respiratory therapist showed me how to read the figures posted on the ventilator. This came in handy when we had our meetings with the doctors as they explained her condition. Also, she was not as swollen since she began dialysis. Initially, her face looked like Joe Frazier's after his battle with Ali at the "Thrilla In Manila." At the same time, we knew she was still with us because her brain CT scans were coming out negative. Unfortunately, both her feet, the fingers including the thumb on the left hand and partially on the fingers on her right hand were dead with gangrene.

One afternoon when I called to check on her status, I was told her left lung had collapsed. I got there as fast as I could to be by her bedside. This time the doctors did not know whether or not she will survive. I signed the consent forms for the surgeon to insert a tube in her left side. Again, the surgeon completed the procedure in her room. The procedure was a success, but she was in very grave condition.

Shortly afterwards, Dr. Chan indicated to us the ventilator tube that went down her throat need to be removed. The tube can be left in her throat for six weeks at the most. Since she needed to remain on the ventilator, a tracheostomy will need to be performed. This is an operation where an opening is cut into the trachea allowing the ventilator to be hooked up. She could remain like this indefinitely.

CHAPTER 7

SERIOUS DECISIONS WITH UNKNOWN CONSEQUENCES

By this time I'm beginning to wonder how much more trauma can her body withstand. Both lungs have collapsed, her limbs are dead, she was constantly dialyzed and she was breathing with the help of a life support machine. Earlier, one of the doctors brought up that since her life style will be changed drastically, would she be able to live with the change. Years ago, she told me she did not want to be kept alive by a machine if she was brain dead. So far her CT scans have been negative. As long as there was life in her brain, we will continue the treatments.

By this time, the doctors were concerned about the condition of her feet and hands. At the same time, the slow process of bringing her out of the coma had begun. She still appeared to be incoherent, but she was able to respond to her name and sometime shake her head yes or no depending on the question. In spite of this step forward, the doctors feared the infection from her left hand began to travel up her arm. Because of this, we were introduced to her vascular surgeon, Dr. Sidney Glaizer.

Another conference was scheduled with the family. The doctors were pleased she was responding to the treatments, but we were not out of the woods, so to speak. In addition to all the medication she was receiving, the doctors began giving her anti anxiety drugs as well. Apparently, Pam was showing some signs of agitation, so now they need to give her something to calm her down. Dr. Glaizer began to describe what they will be doing. In reviewing Pam's case history, the prognosis did not look good. In order to prevent the infection spreading from her left hand, they plan to amputate the left hand. Before doing so, they want to discuss this with her. She was slowly coming out of the coma, but not full coherent. The plan was to cut back on her sedatives so that eventually she would be able to understand what was about to happen.

Lucien had brought up the fact that Pam was such an active person the amputation would be devastating to her. Dr. Glaizer said something to the effect, "If the infection should spread to other organs or systems, it could be fatal." I looked at both Lucien and Doris sensing both were stunned by what the doctor said and was unable to say anything. Eileen broke the silence by asking "Because of the trauma that has occurred, do they plan to do any psychological counseling?" Dr. Chan indicated in due time they will have a psychiatrist check on her. In order to loosen up the seriousness of the situation Eileen said, "With everything that has gone on the entire family will need some type of counseling." No sooner after she said this Doris said, "Don't worry about me. I'm fine and perfectly healthy!" There was dead silence while everybody turned to look at Doris. Eileen and I just looked at each other. I had the feeling Eileen was thinking, "Somebody will need to look after my mother." Doris went on to say, "Just pray to God and He always performs miracles." I'm not one to question one's faith in a Supreme Being, but we are dealing with reality in the face of overwhelming odds.

Once the meeting broke up, I went back to Pam's room. I attempted to ask her a few questions. It appeared she could sense I was in her presence, but she was a bit incoherent. I didn't know whether or not she would be in a position to fully realize the severity of her illness and what the doctors need to do to keep her alive.

A day later, one of the nurses told me they were able to discuss the upcoming amputation. Although she was unable to talk, she wrote on a piece of paper she wanted to live. That was enough for me to go ahead and sign the authorization for the surgery. At first, Dr. Glaizer wanted to do the amputation that evening. Because of the scheduling for use of the operating room, it was decided he would do it the following day. Eileen, Rich and I were aware of this. I decided to keep this from my in-laws. Lucien is in a state of shock and is unable to speak. At the same time, Doris could not fully accept what was happening to her daughter. Early that evening Dr. Glaizer proceeded with the amputation. I waited a full hour until I called

Doris advising the surgery is currently underway. This made her more of a basket case because Lucien was not there to drive her to the hospital (Doris driving was restricted due to health reasons). I did not want them to keep an all night vigil while this was going on. It would be best if we stayed home and pray for the best outcome.

A few hours later, I received a call from Dr. Glaizer indicating the amputation was a success. He went on to say the infection did not spread as far as he thought. Because of this, he was able to save her left hand. All four fingers and the thumb were cut off at the hand. There are pins holding the skin together and now we just wait for it to heal. I thanked him for everything he has done. Shortly afterwards, I received a call from Rich. He happened to be in the area and went in to see how she was doing. She was still out from the anesthesia, but she was in stable condition. Upon hearing this, my mind was at ease and I was able to sleep for more than two hours than what I was accustomed to. I still had concerns regarding Doris' condition.

The following day was the usual routine. Pam was still sedated while her left hand was heavily bandaged and resting on a pillow. She still could not speak due to the trach. A few days later, I received a call from Eileen telling me Pam was fully awake and is doing fine. She was able to write a few things on paper if she had a question. It appears she is going in the right direction. My main concern as well as with the nurses was not letting her know how long she was in a coma. We agreed she would be told in due time. I could not imagine the shock finding out it was the middle of March while the last thing one could remember was it being New Year's Eve.

We kept our first visit fairly simple not knowing her mental state. Eileen happened to be there asking simple questions such as, "Do you know where you are, do you know who I am and do you know this person," while she pointed at me. I could tell she was puzzled why we were treating her like a five year old not knowing the roller coaster ride she had just been on. Pam was told that her fingers and thumb were removed from her left hand. A physical therapist would eventually come to her room having Pam lift her left arm as well as moving it in circles. It was a start, but we knew she had a long way to go.

Approximately ten days later, it was time to change the wrapping and bandage on the left hand. This happened to be a Sunday and Dr. Glaizer was not in. His backup completed this procedure. I happened to be the only visitor there, so this would be an excellent chance to see firsthand (no pun intended) the outcome of the amputation. While removing the bandage, the doctor turned to me asking, "Do you feel faint?" I told him, "While working as a field adjuster there were several occasions I had to inspect cars that were in rather gruesome accidents. I'm immune to blood and guts." He proceeds with the removal of the bandage after giving me a crazy look.

Once the bandage was removed, the remains of the left hand were exposed. Just as Dr. Glaizer explained, the four fingers and thumb were amputated right at the knuckles. Pins were sticking out holding the flesh together. It had a pale white color, but this was a good sign blood was flowing in that area.

I happened to have another meeting with Marcie, the social worker. We were at the point we need to start planning for the future. Should Pam become more stable, she would need to be moved to a skilled nursing facility. I had dollar signs flashing before my eyes thinking I would have to hock everything. Since Pam is now considered permanently disabled, I would have to apply for social security on her behalf. There is a six months waiting period before the initial check is issued, but it would cover the six months retroactive. Time would be of the essence since her unemployment had run out. Also, I would be able to apply for state aid to help cover her stay at the nursing facility. Little did I know what was in store for the next sixteen months.

Applying for social security was fairly easy. Since Pam was unable to do this herself, I went to the nearest social security office and obtained the necessary documents. I advised the workers due to her condition, I may have to sign on her behalf. This should not have been a problem, but just to protect ourselves I had Pam sign the documents to the best of her ability.

Applying for MediCal was a different matter. I had to call the local office and start the process. Once they receive the necessary information over the phone, I was told I would be receiving pamphlets with instructions through the mail. A week later, I received a giant envelope from the Department of Social Services. In short, it would have been easier to apply for a job at the C.I.A. There were all sorts of forms including financial disclosures for the past three years. Some forms read, "If you have children, please complete the questions below. If not, then complete the questions on page such and such." I knew I would have problems obtaining certain information for the allotted time given for me to complete and return. For example, the most recent statement from her credit union might be insufficient due to the fact it came out in the middle of the month and there were holds placed on all withdrawals and deposits. Little did I know this would come back to haunt me in another eighteen months.

As the days passed, Pam was responding favorably with her treatments. Every day the therapist would come in having her go through the exercises to strengthen her left arm. At the same time, the staff began to slowly wean her off the ventilator by cutting back on the pressure. This would help her to start breathing on her own to the point some day she may be off the vent altogether. At first, the respiratory therapist would tell Pam they would cut back on the pressure. For reason unknown, this made Pam anxious to the point she would have panic attacks causing her to pass out. A few times the nursing staff went to get the crash cart thinking she was going into distress to the point she needed to be resuscitated. Eventually, the therapists did not tell her they were cutting back making her think the vent was doing all the work when in fact she was taking steps to breathe on her own.

All during this time, she needed suctioning. Those of you that had family members on a ventilator know what this means. Those who don't, mucus will build up in the lungs and the person may have problems to raise it. What the nurses and respiratory therapists would do is squeeze a small tube of saline solution in order to loosen the mucus. Then, with the aid of a small suction tube the mucus would be vacuumed out of the lungs and up through the throat. It isn't a pleasant sight, but as time went on I got used to watching this procedure.

The doctors also let the therapists manipulate the trach. Once the trach is in place, there is a small balloon that is inflated. This does not allow the air to travel above the sight of the trach. Because of this, the patient is unable to speak or eat. By deflating the balloon, the patient is able to talk and eat soft types of food. For this, Pam had a speech therapist show her how to speak and swallow again. At first, I told her she sounded like Linda Blair from "The Exorcist." Eileen would say, "I bet she could spit out the green slime as well." One has to keep a sense of humor while all this chaos is going on.

Spring of 2003 was well underway. Pam was showing great progress as she was slowly being weaned off the vent. At the same time, she was very anxious in wanting to leave the hospital. This was not an option. Pam still needed intensive rehabilitation. It was not until the end of April the doctors allowed her to go on a small outing. One Sunday afternoon Dr, Chan, her nurse for the day and a respiratory therapist hooked her up to an oxygen tank. She was wheeled through I.C.U. to the back elevator and taken downstairs. From there, she was wheeled to a patio area between the hospital and medical offices. Pam was fairly weak and the sun was too bright for her. I gave her my sunglasses and with that a group picture was taken. Everybody was smiling, but the biggest smile came from Pam. The outing lasted for no more than an hour, but it was a giant step forward in her recovery. Again, we repeated the same process a couple weeks later.

Shortly afterwards, we had another meeting with the staff. Pam was showing such improvement that it was time to move her to a skilled nursing facility. There, she would undergo physical therapy to strengthen her legs for the upcoming bilateral amputation. At first Pam did not like this idea because she wanted to go home. The staff tried to convince her that she is still very ill and will need constant observation. According to Dr. Chan the only way she would be able to go home was to be off the vent for an extended period of time and have the trach permanently removed. It was not until one of the nurses, Neda, sat down and had a long discussion. In short Pam was told there are only two ways she would be able to leave I.C.U. The first would be to move her to one of the rooms downstairs or to a nursing facility. The second option one would have a fairly good idea without going into detail. Pam opted to be moved to New Orange Hills.

CHAPTER 8

NEW LIVING QUARTERS
AND MORE SURGERY

New Orange Hills is located approximately five miles south of the Kaiser Lakeview Medical Center. It is nestled in a residential area just before taking the road up to Irvine Park. It works in conjugation with patients enrolled in the Kaiser program. Three of the pulmonary doctors (Dr. Chan, Dr. Sivjee and Dr. Flatauer) would take turns checking on the Kaiser patients who were on ventilators one day out of the week. There was a large physical therapy room constantly in use throughout the day. Across the hall was a family room with television, computers and pay phones. Further down the hall is the combination dinning activity room. The center of the complex was a patio large enough for tables and chairs should the patients and the families want to soak up the sun or just have a small picnic. There were three sections that housed the patients. Pam would be assigned to the pulmonary unit that housed the patients on ventilators. Both Lucien and Doris had a chance to take a walk through and were pleased with what they saw. I waited until the day Pam was transferred there.

Once transferred by ambulance, Pam was placed in a room with two other roommates. One was Soledad or Sally for short. She had MS and was confined to a wheelchair, but was able to get around. The other was in a feisty mood and passed away a few days later, something one must become accustomed to while at the facility. Unfortunately, the room was very dark in spite of the lighting. Pam complained about this and eventually she was moved to a better room across the hall. The first three months Pam was there, Kaiser would pay for her stay. After that, Social Services would come into play. I was still going through the process trying to get her approval. Some of the information I needed did not come in on time. Because of this, the claim was closed and I had to start all over while filling out the documents and providing the necessary information. At first we did not know how long she needed to stay here. She was looking at the bilateral amputation in the future and returning to New Orange Hills in order to teach her how to walk again. Unknown to me, the nightmare was to begin in a couple months.

After a few days, Pam became used to her new lifestyle. The respiratory therapists were slowly weaning her off the vent. She got to the point she was able to spend short periods of time off the vent and was placed on an oxygen mask. This allowed her to not only move about the hospital, but she was able to have her meals in the dining area, participate in the group activities and most important have her go through the physical and occupational therapies. Friday night was Family Night in that the dietary staff would cook up something special. Everybody would be in the dining room discussing the daily or weekly events. Afterwards, the staff would show a movie on the projected wide screen. Unfortunately, I was unable to participate in the Friday night festivities. I was working at our office located in Corona, some thirty miles north of New Orange Hills. Again, anybody familiar with the Southern California freeway system knows the Friday night commute back to Orange County is a nightmare. At the same time, poor Onslow was getting neurotic on me because of the length of time he was alone each day. Because of this, I would spend Saturday and Sunday visiting Pam. I would use my vacation days by taking a day or two off during the week should she have an appointment to visit the surgeon or just keep her company.

Within the next two months, the physical therapists had Pam walking the halls with the aid of a walker. They also had her riding a stationary bicycle. The staff got her strength built up to the point by July Dr. Glaizer scheduled an appointment to discuss the upcoming bilateral amputation. Initially, Dr. Glaizer wanted to remove one foot and monitor the outcome. If everything went well then the other foot would be removed. Because Pam was so anxious to come home, she pleaded with the doctor asking to have both removed at the same time. Dr. Glaizer eventually gave in. Prior to her amputation, the doctor had to perform a minor procedure. Her right hand did not suffer the same fate as her left hand, but the tip of her right index finger and ring finger were dead with gangrene. The ring finger was in the worst condition. Dr. Glaizer decided to remove the tip as an in office surgery procedure. Initially, the nurses did not want me in the room while the amputation was going on. I attempted to explain blood and guts did not faze me to any avail. A few weeks later during the post-op visit, they allowed me to stay in the room. There wasn't anything exciting in that what the entire doctor did was shoot the hand up with Novocain, make a cut here and there and sew it up. While the tip was placed in a container, my crazy sense of humor came out again, "To bad it wasn't Halloween, I could have put this to good use." Just before we left the office I said, "Don't worry, we will have you walking like Lt. Dan in Forest Gump." Again, one has to keep a sense of humor among the chaos.

July 22, 2003, the date we agreed to have the bilateral amputation. The surgery was scheduled for 10:00 A.M. Because of that, I was at New Orange Hills early before she was transported back to the Lakeview Medical Center. Once she got there, she was taken to the recovery for the out patients. There, we waited until it was time for her to be wheeled to the operating room. While waiting we found out the staff would be removing the trach. Finally, there just might be a light at the end for the tunnel.

As it turns out, the surgery was delayed. Apparently, there was an emergency and all the scheduled operations were pushed back. For the next few hours, all what we could do was watch the portable television that was mounted by the bed. Both Pam's parents were already waiting in the lobby. The only thing I could do was keep them posted. It wasn't until almost 3:00 P.M. before the technicians began to wheel Pam to one of the operating rooms. I followed close behind assuring Pam I'm still with her and everything would be fine. We eventually got to the surgical area and were moved to a combination holding area recovery room. The nurses were checking her charts before wheeling her to one of the operating room just around the corner. She was already groggy from the sedative given to her. When it was time, I held her right hand, kissed my right index finger and pressed it against her lips. As I was leaving the area, I looked upwards and said, "She's now in Your Hands."

I went straight to the lobby and found a comfortable chair. There, both her parents and I kept our vigil. This was about the same time the swing shift was coming on. Doris ran up and greeted the nurses we knew from I.C.U. I don't know what the discussions were about, but one can't say much when a loved one is currently having both feet amputated. I just sat there occasionally closing my eyes just waiting for some good news. Lucien sat there reading a back issue of Newsweek.

Approximately three hours later, the receptionist at the front desk called my name. She had the operator for the surgical ward on the phone. She gave me an update saying the surgery is more than half completed and everything is fine. She isn't loosing much blood and her vital signs were stable. As I went back to my chair I noticed Doris had gotten up to stretch her legs. I proceeded to tell Lucien the status report. After I told him what I knew, he turned to me and asked, "Is there something wrong?" Since Pam was in the coma I noticed Lucien was in a state of shock. He would just sit there staring out not saying anything. One would ask him a question and would either ask to repeat it or give an answer that did not make sense. This time I was telling him everything is fine and he asked me if there was something wrong. With that I decided to go back home to get something to eat. I told the receptionist I would be leaving and have the doctor or nurses call me at home should there be any problems. Later that evening, I spoke to the receptionist at I.C.U. Pam was back in her room resting comfortably.

The following day I went back to work. This may have been a mistake. Late in the morning, I called to check on her status. I was told although her parents were there, she was very anxious. I immediately called my supervisor to see if they could get somebody to cover me for the rest of the day. Once my backup got there I was off to the hospital. I got there and could see she was very anxious in spite of having the morphine pump at her side. The next few hours I attempted to calm her down hoping the morphine will eventually kick in keeping her sedated. With all that morphine she has been taking, she could give Keith Richards a run for the money.

After three weeks Pam was released from the hospital against my wishes. This made me a bit upset because I made it clear I needed advanced warning regarding her release because I need to apply for the family leave. My concern was she was very weak coming off the trach removal to the point she was gasping for air unless she was on an oxygen mask. Also, I was concerned regarding additional physical therapy since both feet have been removed along with the fingers and thumb on the left hand. I was told not to worry because she was being trained how to move herself from the wheel chair to a bed or couch or a commode.

I began the process of applying for the Family Medical leave. Whether I like it or not I was soon to become a caregiver. The paperwork was mailed to me one week after I ordered it. In reviewing the forms I noticed I had fourteen days beginning the day I applied to have the doctor's report in for review. If it wasn't received within the fourteen day period the claim would be denied. Since time was of the essence, I got the paperwork to Marcie at Lakeview and selected a date two weeks in advance to begin the leave. Marcie saw to it that the report was completed and sent out immediately.

It was decided Pam would stay at her parents while I was waiting for the okay for the family leave. Although her father worked part time during the day, her mother helped Pam become accustomed to her new lifestyle. They learned by trial and error on maneuvering the wheelchair and using the transfer board in order for her to get out of the wheelchair. Her left hand and both feet were still heavily bandaged. Dr. Glaizer gave strict instructions that he was the only person to remove the bandages. He was anticipating at least six more weeks before the pins would be removed. Depending on her healing process, she would be looking at the possibility of being fitted for prosthetics. Her parents were very grateful that she had progressed so much. I was worried in trying to get authorization for the time off.

CHAPTER 9

RED TAPE
AND SET BACKS

It was already August of 2003. The last seven months seemed to be a blur, but things appear to be looking up. The only change was I was working at one of our field offices that happened to be much closer to home. My employer had a contest to see if we were able to meet specific goals during the last quarter. Lucky for us, we exceeded it and each employee was given a cash award. A majority of us pooled the money and we chartered a three quarter day fishing boat. At first I did not want to go not knowing if Pam's condition would change. Both my in-laws and especially Pam wanted me to go since I haven't had a break in the action in the last eight months. I decided to go in spite of a gut feeling that something was going to happen.

We all had a great time spending a workday fishing off the Southern California coast. Most of us were catching our limit of sand bass while others spent time feeding the fish. I did okay knowing we will have a good size fish fry once I got back home. This day off seemed to do wonders for me.

I got back home early in the evening. After packing the fish in the freezer and cleaning the equipment I went to take a long shower. There were messages on the recorder. The first one was my father-in-law. He started off, "I have some bad news for you." My heart sunk to my stomach with a great big thud. Lucien indicated Pam had to be rushed to the hospital after passing out. The second message was Lucien again indicating they are attempting to stabilize her. The third call was Eileen telling me to call her immediately.

I got in contact with Eileen. In short, Pam had to be intubated and placed back on a ventilator. What had happened, since Pam was release, Kaiser had a home health nurse come in and check on her every other day. The nurse would check her vital signs and administer any medications as needed. What happened was Pam was very lethargic when the nurse came to my in-laws home. While being examined, Pam just passed out. Without wasting any time, they contacted the paramedics to get her to the nearest emergency room. Upon arriving at Whittier Community Hospital, the staff was completely puzzled by her condition. No one there had seen anybody in the condition that Pam was in. They could not understand why someone in her condition was released to go home.

Eileen immediately got to the emergency room. Sensing they were short of writing Pam off she immediately called Dr. Sivjee and explained what was going on. Dr. Sivjee asked to speak to the physician in charge. Again, as luck would have it both doctors had crossed paths at one time or another. It was agreed to have Pam stabilized and moved by ambulance with a physician present back to Lakeview.

Pam eventually woke up in I.C.U. at Lakeview later that evening. Immediately, she notices she was on the vent since the trach was removed. She remained on the vent for two days before placed on oxygen via a nasal canula. She remained there for two weeks before being transferred back to New Orange Hills. She stayed at New Orange Hills to give her more confidence on her breathing. All during this time, I was still waiting for the authorization for the family leave while spinning my wheels providing the necessary documentation for the Social Services Department.

Tuesday August 19, 2003, the day all hell broke loose. I was already back to work after taking a week off for my birthday. It was business as usual at the field office. There would be situations I would be outside of the office nowhere near a phone. Because of this, I made sure the hospital staff at both Lakeview and New Orange Hills had my pager number. Late that morning, the pager went off indicating someone at New Orange Hills was trying to contact me. I called and it turned out to be one of the discharge planners telling me Pam was ready to be released and wanted to know when I will be picking her up. This made me a bit upset because I made it clear I will need some advanced warning as to when she would be released so I could advise my employer for the family leave. Besides, she still had some time left for Kaiser to pay for her stay at New Orange Hills. It was as if the discharge planner ignored what I said and repeated the fact Pam was going to be discharged and when will I be there to pick her up. I told her something to the effect that I'm not in a position to do so because I'm here at work until late this afternoon and I'm still waiting for the authorization for the family leave. After going around in circles, I told the planner I will get back to her later this afternoon.

I immediately contacted Marcie at Lakeview and explained to her the situation with New Orange Hills. I expressed my reservations about her release based on what happened a couple weeks ago. Also, although the trach had been removed, Pam was gasping for air every time she speaks. Marcie told me there wasn't much they could do. Once they plan to discharge her, the decision is final.

At this point I knew we could not move Pam back to her parent's home. Her father was still working during the day. Her mother was seventy-five years old. Prior to this happening, Doris was caring for Pam's paternal grandmother for the last two or three years without any help from the family. She would be running around tending to her needs during her waking hours. This lasted until six weeks prior to Pam becoming sick when her grandmother passed away. The last eight months took a toll on Doris. By the time Pam had to be returned to the hospital, one could tell that Doris was hurting physically and mentally. I made a decision that going back to her home was not an option.

I purposely waited until late in the afternoon knowing the discharge planner would be gone for the day before I called her back. She returned my call the following day. I gave her the reasons why I felt I was not in a position to bring Pam home. I emphasized the fact that I was still waiting for the authorization for the family leave. I was told in no uncertain terms I did not have a say in her release. After our heated conversation went around in circles, the planner requested that I discuss this further with the Kaiser doctor on duty.

Shortly afterwards, I received a call from the attending physician. Calmly, I went over the reason I felt I was not in a position to bring Pam home. She went on to say Pam has been stabilized and has been trained how to move around while at home. I told her she does not understand. On short notice, I can't just pick her up and drop her off at either her parents' residence or back home. At the same time I requested the staff to notify me ahead of time as to her release date so that I would be able to finalize the process of applying for the family leave, something that I'm still waiting for. The doctor caught me off guard by telling me, "You should have known this day was coming."

"Not without advanced warning," I shouted back.

Unless you have something constructive to say this conversation is over," she snapped back.

This stunned me for a few seconds. "I'm not in a position to bring her home!"

I could hear she was hanging up on me. By this time I was so angry that with the receiver to my ear I said something to the effect, "You unintelligent female dog!" To this day I'm not sure whether or not she heard me.

After regaining my composure, I contacted my immediate supervisor advising him of the situation and that I will need the rest of the day off in order to bring Pam home. I will remain off until I get the authorization for the family leave. I then left a message with the discharge planner advising her I will be picking up Pam later this afternoon. All during this time neither Pam nor her parents had any idea what was going on.

I got to New Orange Hills later that afternoon and noticed my in-laws were already there. Wednesdays were usually set aside for them to visit Pam during the course of the week. By now, I was sure they were aware of all the commotion that had occurred and decided to wait until I got there. I walked through the entrance straight to her room. Without saying hello I asked, "Are you ready to leave this shit box?" Both her parents were in the room as well as the nurse that was giving Pam instructions. They knew I was a force not to be messed with.

Before we could leave, we had to wait for the hospital to contact a medical supply company to bring equipment to the home. The main item was a concentrator. This was a device that manufactures oxygen while the patient wears a nasal canula. This can go on indefinitely as opposed to using an oxygen tank. One oxygen tank can last anywhere from ninety minutes to two hours depending on the amount flowing. They still had to bring us oxygen tanks as well. Also needed was a bedside commode. The deliveries can be made twenty-four hours a day. These were to be delivered shortly after I brought Pam home. The plan was I would bring Pam home in our 97 Camaro along with a wheelchair. Her parents would bring her personal belongings.

As we were pulling up to our condo complex, I'm thinking to myself, "Now the fun begins." The condo complex is tri-leveled with a number of stairs leading from the parking lots to the walkways that leads to each unit.

There was only one incline that would lead to the walkway leading to our unit. The problem was there were three steep steps at the end. I went to one of our neighbors, Cheryl and her brother Mike. The plan was Cheryl will stand at our front door while it was open. I had Mike walk Onslow in the opposite direction so that he would not see what was going on. After eight months of not seeing Pam, I thought Onslow would go bonkers once he would see her.

The incline was wide enough to accommodate the wheelchair. This was taking in account she had a holding device mounted to the back that would carry her oxygen tank. I had to pull her backwards until we got to the three stairs. There, I angled the wheelchair having the front wheels up in the air while using the two large wheels to pull her up the steps. Once at the top I was able to turn the wheelchair around and just push her to our unit. Once we got there, we immediately saw the wheelchair would not fit through the entry. At the same time I saw our condo unit would not be able to accommodate the wheelchair at all. The only thing I could do was carry Pam to the couch while Cheryl followed close behind with the oxygen tank. There, Pam would remain until she was able to walk with her prosthetic legs up the stairs to our bedroom. Once I made her comfortable, I signaled Mike to bring Onslow in. Just as I guessed, he went bananas once he saw Pam. It was very hard for me to hold back the tears.

Some of the neighbors saw me wheel Pam past their units. For the next hour, they would stop by to pay their respects. Most of them pulled me to the side asking should she be home because she was gasping for air while she spoke. I told them it was a touchy issue since I did not have any say on her release. In spite of her gasping for air, Pam was very happy talking to our neighbors.

Shortly afterwards, the medical supply company came by dropping off the necessary equipment. They made it clear should she use up her oxygen tanks to just call anytime during the day and they would bring her fresh ones. My main concern was the concentrator. This was a fifty pound machine on wheels that had all sorts of dials on it. Pam was already trained on how to use it and gave me a crash course on how it works. Next, I had stacks of paperwork to go over. Some was instructions on her diet. Also, I had documents regarding dialysis. She had to continue her three time a week sessions. Since she is now considered permanently disabled. She could qualify to be transported to and from the nearest outpatient dialysis center. This was already arranged with the Orange County Transit

Authority before she left New Orange Hills. I just needed to contact them to schedule when she would be picked up on Friday.

As the evening went on I could tell she was exhausted from her trip back home. As luck would have it, we have a downstairs bathroom. Again, because our unit could not accommodate the wheelchair, I would carry her and place her on a chair in front of the sink. Although it was not her own bed, she was comfortable being on the couch. Because she was gone for so long, Onslow would snuggle against her and would not leave her side the entire evening. I gave her a bell so that if she needed anything during the course of the evening, she would ring it signaling me to come downstairs. I too was worn out after what transpired during the course of the day. I vaguely recall my head hitting the pillow and then the lights went out.

The following day I was up early to begin the first day of being a caregiver. Pam ringed for me only once so I did have a restful evening. I would cook up her breakfast and then tend to her while scrubbing up in the sink. One thing I did not have to worry about was her hair. Pam has natural curly hair that came down to the middle of her back. During the time she was in a coma, the staff was ready to write her off. Because of that, they did not tend to her hair. When she came to, the least problem was her hair, it was all matted. As much as we did not want to, it was decided her hair would be cut short and eventually it would grow out back to the same condition.

Later that morning, I received a call from the home health nurse. They would be coming out later today to check on Pam. Once he got there, he checked her vital signs making sure her oxygen levels were within the excellent range. We already made the arrangements for her to be picked up tomorrow afternoon to be taken in for her dialysis session. The only drawback was after each session, Pam would need to be given an injection of Procrit. Pam was very exhausted after each dialysis session. In order to build her cells up she was given an injection of Procrit. Of course, I would have to administer the injection. I'm not very fond of shots and I think giving them is not my cup of tea. It would come down to me giving her the injection once she returned home from the session. Knowing that I would be a terrible junkie I asked the nurse if someone at the outpatient unit would be able to give her the injection. He was not sure because these units do not keep a stock of medications for the patients. It is possible I may have to bring a vial of Procrit and see if one of the nurses or technicians would be able to give the injection. If not, it would be up to me.

Later that afternoon, I had to go shopping to stock up the home. I knew it would be a challenge because of the restrictions on her diet. I had Mike come over to stay with Pam while I went shopping. I figured while I was out, she could catch up with what was happening in Cheryl's and Mike's life over the past eight months. After about three hours and two stores I finally had enough for the next few days. That evening, we spent a quite night watching television. Pam ringed me only once during the evening. She was having some pain, so I gave her a painkiller.

Friday August 22, 2003, day number two that Pam was home. Everything started out just like yesterday, except for the fact Pam appeared to be very groggy. I figured out it must have been the effects of the painkiller I gave her in the middle of the night. It took some coaxing, but I eventually got her up. She claims she felt very tired and just wanted to sleep. She eventually allowed me to place her on the wheelchair at the dinner table and proceeded to make her breakfast. She was very lethargic and barley ate half her breakfast. I wanted to take her to the bathroom so could clean herself up. She insisted I take her back to the couch. I figured to let her sleep for at least an hour before I made an attempt for her to have a midmorning snack. I placed her on the concentrator and kept an eye on the volume she was receiving while I sat next to her.

An hour later I attempted to wake her up. "Come on Pammy, we need to get you going because you have dialysis later this afternoon." She just lay there motionless but still breathing. Again, I tried calling her, but did not get a response. I gave her a little shove and again called her name. She then turned towards me as her eyes rolled up into her head. "Oh shit, it is time to call 911!" What transpired next was a page out of some black comedy skit. I proceeded to call 911 explaining what is going on. "Let me speak to her," the person on the other end asked. I stood there stunned wondering why she would ask such a question. "No, you don't understand. She is extremely lethargic but still breathing. I attempted to wake her, but her eyes rolled up back into her head. It is safe to say she is unconscious, but still breathing."

"Let me speak to her," the person on the other end requested. I began to remember a situation similar to this that occurred in Texas a few years ago. What happened was a son called 911 saying his mother was having a heart attack. The person on the other end kept on asking to speak to the mother. The son was very agitated screaming his mother is having a heart attack and they need someone out there now. The operator said something to the effect don't use that tone of voice at me and let me speak to your mother. After going around in circles, the son ended the conversation by saying something to the effect, "I hope you're happy because you just killed my mother," and hung up. Needless to say, the mother did not survive and a complaint was filed. The operator was fired from the job, but she did the All American duty by filing a wrongful termination suit and became rich. I'm now dealing with a moron following in the same footsteps.

"Please listen to me carefully. I'm going to attempt to place the receiver in my wife's hand so you can speak to her," I told the operator. I attempted to prop Pam's right arm up so that she could hold the receiver. Three times I placed it in her right hand and three times the receiver fell between her and the upright rest of the couch. I got on the lie and said, "The noise you just heard was the receiver falling from my wife's hand down on the couch. I am fairly certain she is unconscious now." I said this with the utmost self control because I could feel the veins bulging from my neck.

"I will send the paramedics immediately. If you have a dog, please see that it is out of the way when they get there," she told me. Unknown to me, this living nightmare was about to become worst.

It seemed like an eternity before the paramedics arrived. During that time, I coaxed Onslow into his cage by throwing a biscuit. After that, I sat by Pam calling out her name. Sometime she would respond by turning her head to the direction I was calling from, but not much after that. I could hear the sirens in the distance gradually growing louder. I began to think to myself, "And to think two days ago I was told I should have expected this coming." I wish that doctor was standing here now to see Pam's condition and ask me if I had anything constructive to say. The only thing I had to say now was again references to biology, family ancestry and religion.

The team of paramedics finally arrived. Two of them immediately went straight to Pam and began to take her vital signs. I was giving another paramedic her vital information. I attempted to explain what occurred the past few days, but not before giving the background of the past few months. Meanwhile, the paramedics were calling Pam's name and asking general questions such as what day is it and do you know where you are. Again, she turned towards the paramedics with her eyes open, but they immediately rolled back into her head. By that time I was told she was in serious condition and needed to be moved to the nearest emergency room. I requested that she be moved to the Lakeview Medical Center. I was told her condition is too serious that she should be moved to the nearest emergency room. That would be Anaheim Memorial, less than two miles from our home. I told them to go ahead and move her there while they had me sign authorizations.

"I should have expected this coming," I kept hearing in my mind. I wanted to call the doctor at New Orange Hills and ask, "Does this include the fact you knew she was going to die without the benefit of warning me?" Nobody on the face of the earth could determine the hatred I had towards that doctor and the staff at New Orange Hills.

Once they wheeled Pam into the ambulance, I called the Transit Authority to cancel the pickup and any other future pick up because Pam was on her way back to the hospital. I then went to our neighbor, Mike, and asked if he could look in on Onslow later on because I did not know if and when I would be coming home. With that, I was immediately off to Anaheim Memorial wondering if this would be a long vigil or worse.

I got to the front desk at the emergency room and identified myself. I asked when I could go back where they currently have Pam. The receptionist called back to the emergency desk. She told me I would have to wait a few minutes before they let me back there. I sat in the waiting room with mixed emotions with hatred towards New Orange Hills and concern whether or not Pam will survive.

A few minutes later I was allowed back in the emergency area. As expected, I was filling out forms while one of the nurses was asking questions on why she was brought there. She was already hooked up to monitors, oxygen via a nasal canula and began running all kinds of blood test. I just sat there in the cubicle where they had Pam and just watched the monitors. By this time, I was able to read the monitors and figure out how she was doing. It did not require a technician to determine she wasn't well.

An hour later, the attending physician spoke to me. She went on to say that pancreatitis has a tendency to reoccur and can be fatal. Right now her oxygen saturation level is low and she has a urinary infection. They began liquid antibiotics and are attempting to stabilize her. A call has gone out for an acute specialist to look at her. She asked if I had any questions. I sat there motionless staring off into space. She then expressed that I looked angry. Angry? I've been through hell for the last eight months, the nursing home kicks her out and now she is within a heartbeat of being placed on life support again! The doctor understood this was a trying experience and suggested if I want to have her transferred here at Anaheim Memorial for the duration of her sickness. I told her no, just go with the plan to stabilize her and then we can transfer her back to Lakeview.

I figured I better let the rest of the family know what is going on. I contacted Lucien on his cell phone saying Pam was unconscious, that she is at the emergency room at Anaheim Memorial and they are trying to stabilize her. I don't know if it was a bad connection or he was still stunned as to what was going on, but he repeated back, "Oh, she is conscious and is doing fine?" I sat there dumbfounded and began to repeat what I had already told him. This time he replied, "She is at the hospital and is stabilized." I took a deep breath and held it for a few seconds before I made my third attempt. I told him, "Pam had to be rushed to the nearest emergency room. She is unconscious and in serious condition. The staff is working to stabilize her before attempts will be made to move her back to Lakeview." There was a moment of silence. Lucien indicated he will pick up Doris and meet me here.

I sat in the cubicle watching the clock and monitors. If I knew better, it appeared her vital signs were dropping. All during this time a nurse did not come in to check her monitors. A couple times I went to the desk telling them they may want to check her vital signs. Each time I was told it would be a matter of time when the ambulance will be there to move her to Lakeview. I just sat there watching her blood pressure, respiration and oxygen saturation levels drop. I started to become very concerned because her vital signs were worse now as opposed to when she got to the emergency room. By 4:00 P.M. the ambulance arrived. The driver took one look at the monitors and said, "We can't move her in this condition!" Immediately, a nurse ran into the cubicle yelling, "Call respiratory!" Another nurse grabbed me by the arm telling me, "We are going to intubate her." Great, they are placing her back on the ventilator. I was escorted back to the waiting room. There I sat while steam was escaping from my ears.

A few minutes later I was allowed back to her cubicle. The only difference now was the tube protruding from her mouth that was pumping oxygen that kept her alive. Again, the attending physician told me they are waiting for the acute specialist to see what our next plan would be. Needless to say, transferring her back to Lakeview tonight was out of the question. One of the nurses came up to me indicating my in-laws were in the waiting room. I went back to the waiting room and told them what happened this morning and what has already been done to this point. Again, Doris came out with her ongoing saying, "It is in God's hands and He works miracles every day." Maybe so, but the idiots at New Orange Hills had surely goofed (not the exact expression used) this time. Shortly afterwards, Eileen walked in at which time I explained everything to her.

The next couple hours seemed to take forever. To our surprise, Rich eventually came to the waiting room. Apparently he got one of his neighbors to look after the two boys and came down here. The five of us just sat there watching the time waste away. She was showing signs of recognizing us, but was still very groggy.

Finally, the acute specialist came in. After reading over her charts he asked what led up to her being brought to the emergency room. I gave him the complete run down starting from day one until the paramedics brought her here. He was rather surprised I was able to give him precise information. He asked, "You were very thorough. Did you have any medical training in the past?"

"No," I answered. "I have seen so much done to her that I probably could breeze through the first two years of med school."

The doctor felt the pancreatitis may have returned, but not to the same degree when she initially came down with it. The doctor decided to order a series of X-Rays and CT scans. This took about an hour before she was brought back to the emergency room. He went on to discuss what they plan to do. She will remain at Anaheim Memorial in I.C.U. overnight. He will order to start up a platelet pherisis session. Immediately, something went off in my mind. "He is aware all of this started with the acute pancreatitis and there is a possibility it may have returned. If this is the case, why then did the staff at Lakeview wait for almost six weeks before they started the platelet pherisis sessions?"

I told the doctor she has already gone through fourteen of those sessions. He thought out loud they might hold off on that. What they will do is immediately start up a dialysis session since she was scheduled for one earlier in the day. This usually took 2.5 hours to complete. Since it was already dark outside and one can't get excited watching blood flowing through the tubes in and out of the machine we decided we would leave for the evening. I told Pam good night and I would see her tomorrow. I had a feeling she knew I was talking to her, but she could not fully comprehend what was going on.

I got back home and saw Mike was with Onslow. He already fed him and just took him out on an evening walk. In the meantime, I went to pick up the mail. Among the bills and the letters telling me we have been pre-approved for a credit card with a $50,000.00 limit there was a letter from the family leave unit. In short it said I was authorized to begin the leave on August 22, 2003. About the same time the age old question went through my mind, "Aside from the shooting, how did you like the play, Mrs. Lincoln?"

Early the next morning, I received a call from Doris. She wanted to know if I have already called over to Anaheim Memorial checking on Pam's status. I was moving around slowly after what happened yesterday. After telling her no, she went on to tell me Pam's room number in I.C.U. and the name of the nurse who will be tending to her. I spent most of the day sitting just staring off into space. I decided I will still take the time off since I had a feeling Pam's release to come home has been placed on an indefinite hold.

It has been said all through the tragedy there is some good. This is what happened when Pam wound up at Anaheim Memorial. Pam had a friend named Eileen Wilson that graduated the same year from La Mirada High. Both kept in touch even after both were married. Unfortunately, Eileen had some rough times and both of them lost contact. To Pam's surprise Eileen was working the switchboard at Anaheim Memorial. The way she found out was when Doris called to find out about Pam, Eileen happened to take the call and something went off in her mind. Sure enough, it turned out to be the same person.

Later that afternoon, I went to visit Pam. Upon entering her room, she was still intubated and could not talk. There was a clipboard with paper and a pencil for her to communicate. Her eyes were wide open as if she was asking, "What happened?" I don't want to know what happened yesterday. She kept on writing, "Please tell me." I went ahead and told her everything what I knew. She just sat there as if she could not believe that happened to her. Later on, the nurse came by and filled me in as to what was going on. She does have a urinary infection and is receiving antibiotics. Her oxygen saturation level was low causing her to go unconscious. Since she has been on the vent the levels have gone up to the excellent range. It is possible she may be moved back to Lakeview later today, but that was pending the attending physician's decision. I just sat there keeping Pam company. Late in the afternoon I was already home and received a call from Lucien. They were in the process of moving Pam back to Lakeview. There she would remain until the beginning of October.

CHAPTER 10

"WHAT WE HAVE HERE . . ."

The next six weeks were rather uneventful. Pam was back in the same room in I.C.U. and all the familiar faces were tending to her. They monitored her infection and continued her dialysis sessions three times a week. She was placed on oxygen via a nasal canula, but her lungs were very weak. The pulmonary doctors decided to perform another tracheostomy and place her back on a ventilator. Again, until she was able to get to levels that she was breathing on her own, but she was unable to speak. This put a damper on her. By this time a number of her friends had found out what happened to her. Most of them were able to visit her. This was able to cheer her up.

The meetings with the staff continued. Sensing that Doris was having problems to cope, it was decided we would continue these meetings without her parents. This was a good decision because by the beginning of October talk began about moving her back to a skilled nursing facility. It didn't surprise me that New Orange Hills refused to accept her back. Again, the discharge planner said a facility can refuse to accept any patient without a reason. I had a fairly good idea why they did not want her back. The problem was Pam needed to be at a skilled facility that not only was able to accommodate her on a ventilator, but also perform bedside dialysis. It turns out the closest was Reche Canyon Center all the way out in Colton. To give one a perspective how far this was, it is exactly eight miles from our home to the Lakeview Medical Center. I discovered it was exactly fifty miles from our home to the driveway that led to Reche Canyon Rehab Center. Pam was furious when she found out about this. She really did not have

52

any say as to where she wanted to go. Again, I had to start all over with Social Services on filling out the paperwork this time using Reche Canyon as her nursing facility.

Pam was transferred on October 9. I was already back at work and visiting her everyday was out of the question. It was decided I would visit her every Saturday. Her parents would visit her every Saturday and Sunday. It turns out Reche Canyon was much fancier than New Orange Hills. They didn't have much in the way of activities like New Orange Hills, but they did have a physical therapy room not as large as her previous facility. They did have an inhouse movie channel hooked up to a DVD player. She was able to catch up on plenty of movies that she missed over the past few months. Aside from that, she wasn't very happy there. She had the feeling that Reche Canyon was a location to perform community service. The reason was all the female CNA's had more than one tattoo. She was expecting a gang war to break out at any time.

I was not exactly happy of the one hundred mile round trip I was faced with every Saturday. One would expect traffic would be light on the weekends. Not so! The route I took was basically the same route one would take to Las Vegas. Also, there was road construction going on in the Riverside area that served as a delay. My patience was put to the test when massive brush fires broke out. It was as if a giant cloud of smoke would cover the freeway for a number of miles. The smoke was so thick I had to slow down to 30 M.P.H. while driving with the headlights on. Regardless of my dislike for this, I made the drive every Saturday. I would discuss the week's happenings while Pam told me how she would spend her day. This was the routine for the next couple months.

Thanksgiving was spent rather low key. I got there in time so the both of us were able to catch the last half of the Macy's Thanksgiving Day Parade, something Pam insists on watching every year. The hospital staff cooked up a Thanksgiving Day luncheon. Pam was not in a position to eat in the dining room yet, so we had the cafeteria bring me a tray and the both of us had Thanksgiving dinner in her room. It wasn't fancy, but it would do based on the circumstances we were faced with

During this time, I was in contact with one of Pam's best friend, Joanne Compton. She would call from Oklahoma wanting to know the status and progress of Pam's convalesce. I would fill her in as to what was going on. A majority of the time there wasn't any change. Latter on she indicated she would be coming out to visit her family over the Thanksgiving Holiday and wanted to see Pam. She kept me posted as to when she will be out. It was decided I would take her the day after Thanksgiving. Of course, I did not tell Pam what was going on. The day finally came as to when I took Joanne out to Reche Canyon.

At first I told Joanne to wait outside Pam's room so that I could check if she was awake or they had her doing something. I got in there and told Pam to close her eyes until I told her to open them. She did and I had Joanne come in. After Pam opened her eyes, it took a few seconds for it to register that Joanne had come out to visit her. The both of them were hugging each other like two long lost sisters. Again, it was hard to hold back the tears.

Christmas was just around the corner and needless to say nobody was in a festive mood. Christmas shopping was not an option, let alone what to buy and for whom. Just as we thought she was becoming stabilized, Pam began bleeding into the tracheostomy. At first, the staff was not alarmed. She had a tendency doing this while at Lakeview. The doctors would go in with a small scope to check the source of the bleeding. Once found, the source of the bleeding would be cauterized. This particular day, she was passing fresh blood all day long. Finally, she was transferred to the Kaiser Medical Center in Riverside, approx fifteen miles south of Reche Canyon. This was on the 9th, I received a call during the evening from the nursing staff at Reche Canyon and was told Pam was being transferred because of her bleeding. Unfortunately, they were unable to tell me what time she would arrive there. I immediately notified my in-laws. It was decided they would go out to Riverside the following day. Again, I had to wait until I got back to work to move around my schedule because I was going to have some time off for at least the last two weeks for the Christmas Holiday. Riverside was not as far as Reche Canyon, but there would be traffic during certain hours.

The doctors decided to perform a fiber optic laryngoscopy. A small wire with a camera on the end is inserted into the lungs. This allows the doctors to see if anything is going on within the lungs. Unfortunately, neither ulceration nor any source of bleeding was found. It was discovered she was suffering from pneumonia and the blood in the trach sight was secondary. This, along with a urinary infection, the doctors had her on massive doses of antibiotics. Her white cell count was on the rise, but it eventually leveled off after Christmas.

Christmas Day finally arrived. Surprisingly, the traffic was not that bad going out there. I got there as soon as visiting hours began. Unlike last year,

Pam was spending Christmas Day in I.C.U. Her parents got there about one hour later and stayed for a short time. They left and went straight to Eileen's to celebrate with a Christmas Dinner. I was to go straight there once I left. As luck would have it, Pam was scheduled for dialysis that same day. Within thirty minutes into the session she went to sleep because she was extremely weak. Great, I can hear it now, "What did you do for Christmas?"

"I watched blood flow in and out of a machine that kept Pam alive."

I stayed until after the dialysis session. Pam was so weak it was difficult for her to remain awake. I stayed for a bit longer and then decided to leave for Eileen's home. This was a mistake. It started to rain and unknown to me it was the beginning of the Great Storm of Christmas 2003. At the same time a short distance from the hospital were the killer mudslides in the areas that just had the recent brush fires. The rain was coming down in sheets making it difficult to see past the hood. In short, what should have taken me only thirty to forty minutes to get back home took me just over two hours. I called Eileen and she understood I did not want to slosh around anymore today.

The next few days Pam's condition improved greatly. During the day she was able to stay on similar to a nasal canula. At night, she would be hooked up to the ventilator. The setting would be low enough that she would be breathing on her own, but every time after she inhaled the vent was set to give that little puff of air if she needed it. This continued until the 29th of December when the doctors decided to move her back to Reche Canyon.

New Years 2004 rolled in low key as well. Driving out to Colton on New Year's Eve was out of the question. Half of Southern California would be on the road to Las Vegas to take part in the festivities and Pam knew this. She did not want me out on the road with all the whackos for the next few days. Because of this, I waited until the following Saturday to go out there.

As luck would have it, the New Year did not start off on the right foot. I was still battling with Social Services for state approval for the benefits to cover her stay at Reche Canyon. A couple requests came up that I was unable to provide the necessary information. This had to do with Pam's personal IRA. Basically, all the funds had to be liquidated, but the signed power of attorney that I was using was unacceptable to the bank. Again, I had to start all over by producing the necessary documents and figure out how to resolve the matter on the IRA.

After a couple weeks into the New Year, I received a message on my pager to call Reche Canyon. According to the nursing staff, Pam's oxygen levels were low and she was exhibiting signs of another infection. They had to rush her back to Kaiser in Riverside. Once again, I called my supervisor so he could get someone to cover for me. I immediately left for Riverside. Once I got there I was allowed into the emergency room where Pam was being monitored. She was coherent and I ask, "Are you okay?"

"Yes, I'm alright," she replied lethargically. She sat there for the next few minutes looking as if she was whacked out on morphine again. I asked, "Are you sure you are alright?"

"Yes," she said, "but I'm trying to talk to the lady in the bed next to mine." I don't know if she was hallucinating or she was having an out of the body experience and talking to the spirits but she was the only person in that area of the emergency room. I pointed this out to her to no avail. About the same time she began to pass blood into the trach.

After a while, the attending physician came by asking me questions of her current medical history. I explained what has occurred over the past year. I was told the oxygen levels were low and her white cell count was very high. It was decided she would be admitted for further treatment. There really wasn't much I could do so I called my in-laws advising them what is going on and she will be back at Kaiser in Riverside.

The following Saturday was a day I would like to forget. My in-laws were already at I.C.U. by the time I got there. Eileen arrived shortly after me. While we were all there, I was introduced to Dr. Francesca Adriano, who was in charge of Pam's case. Unknown to me she was in charge of Pam's case last month as well. My first impression was she did not look any older than my youngest cousin on my father's side of the family, Mary Kim. I don't think she was 36 years old at the time. Oh well, if you have a pipeline to money and graduate at the head of your class, more power to you. During this stay I notice Pam had a close bond with Dr. Adriano.

Once she saw we were all there, she began to give us an update similar to what we were accustomed back at Lakeview. She went on to say Pam had a very bad infection and was being treated with massive doses of antibiotics. At the same time, they were attempting to control the bleeding with other medication. All through the discussion Dr. Adriano had a somber tone as if the outcome was not good. She ended the conversation by saying Pam will remain in I.C.U. for further observation and treatment.

All during this time Pam was semiconscious. I'm certain she did not hear, let alone understand what was going on. No sooner when Dr. Adriano finished, Doris went to Pam's bedside, began to brush her hair and told her, "You see, the doctors will make you well so that you will be coming home soon." Everybody sat there stunned. Dr. Adriano's eyes were about to pop out while her jaw hit the ground. Eileen immediately got into her mother's face saying, "That is not what she said and you know it!" I sat there hoping the nightmare would go away. I was too shocked to hear the rest of Eileen's exuberant discussion with her mother.

Shortly afterwards, Fr. Andrew happened to stop by. I was surprised to see him since it was a rather long drive from south Orange County all the way out to Riverside. He took a seat and began some small talk with Pam's parents. I just sat there wondering if Doris would become unglued at the seams. One thing led to another that both Fr. Andrew and Lucien began talking about the current football playoffs. When asked what team did Lucien think will win the Super Bowl he replied, "I hope Green Bay will go all the way." Fr. Andrew and I just looked at each other. "Green Bay played last week and lost," he told Lucien.

"Oh," was the only reply coming from Lucien. Again, it scared me. I did not know if he heard the question or if he was in such a state of shock he did not understand. During my drive back home I wondered what else is in store for me.

If there was a way to avoid the month of February I was all for it. I was a basket case pushing myself each day knowing Pam was back in I,C.U. and the medical staff is ready to write her off. I was still dealing with Social Services not knowing if and when Pam would be eligible for state funds. To make matters worse, I started receiving calls from the business office at Reche Canyon. They were inquiring about when they will be receiving our co-payments. One night I received a call from Eileen. She was able to visit Pam and was able to communicate with her. In short, Pam wanted out before they killed her. She went on to say the staff went as far as asking if she was afraid to die! This was during the beginning of the month and she wasn't in any shape to be transferred.

Finally, one day turned into the day from hell. I was working at the field office in Anaheim and throughout the day I had laptop problems. I had to remain there after hours for a couple of supervisors to come out to see if they could correct the problem. During the course of the day, I was still receiving calls from the business office at Reche Canyon. While they were working on my laptop I was paged by the business manager at Reche Canyon. I took the call in another room and closed the door knowing this might get nasty. In short, he was looking for the co-payment and requested I drive out there tonight and deliver it. We are talking about $7,980.00. Anybody familiar with the freeway system is quite aware the evening drive from Anaheim to the Inland Empire is fairly close to gridlock. If I was able to leave now I would be looking at a three hour drive to travel just over fifty miles. He then asked if I could wire him the money now. Again, I said I was not in a position to do this. He threw some gasoline on the fire by asking why not. I blew up at him saying I have done everything short of walking on water and I'm still waiting for Social Services to come through. Seeing that we were not getting anything accomplished, I abruptly ended the conversation saying I will get back to him. No sooner I hung up my pager went off again. This time it was a discharge planner from Kaiser in Riverside. In short, he told me Pam might be released very shortly and wondered why I was unable to get the matter with Social Services resolved. To this day I do not recall what was said but this character had to deal with me while I was going ballistic.

After that conversation, I went back to the room where they were working on my laptop. The two of them took a quick glance at me then continued to work on the laptop. I'm quite sure they heard the yelling going on in the other room. Just as they were finishing up, in walked two Anaheim Police officers. The two supervisors asked if they need any help and the officers just said no. They wanted to speak to me alone after we were finished. "Great," I'm thinking to myself. "What in the hell did I do now?"

The two officers pulled up a chair just as the two supervisors were leaving the office. They asked me my name, my address and a few other things. I answered them and asked why all of this? Apparently, the discharge planner was afraid I was going to commit suicide and immediately called the Anaheim PD. They kept me there for the next two hours while I told them everything that has been going on. They would not leave until I promised them I would not kill myself and I would contact a priest. The discharge planner does not know the anger I had towards him. What was more embarrassing was the two supervisors waited in the parking lot until we left the building. Again, the two supervisors asked if there was anything they could do. The officers replied everything is under control. I proceeded to go home where I drank my dinner of Chardonnay.

The next few weeks I was running around like an idiot. My concentration level was so low it started to affect my work. The supervisors started getting on my case on the poor quality I was turning out. One day my immediate supervisor left a lengthy message on my voicemail. He happened to be one of the supervisors at the field office when the two officers from the Anaheim Police Department came in to pay their respects. He was aware of what was going on and was very concerned. He indicated to call him anytime so that we can talk and hopefully resolve my problems. I appreciated what he has done for me since this all started, but I'm at a point that my life is a living nightmare and it will not go away.

My family members began to notice the toll this had taken on me. I could not tell Pam everything what was going on let alone get my family involved in my battles with Social Services and the facilities business offices. Pam could see the despair in my face every time I visited her. We knew sooner or later everything would fall into place, but the way things were going, it might take something short of divine intervention.

By the end of February, Pam had dramatically become stable for her condition. It was time to move her back to Reche Canyon. At first I thought we would run into problems with the business office, but so far I did not hear from them. Each time I visited Pam at Reche Canyon I kept a low profile so that an administrator or discharge planner would not see me.

When she was moved back to Reche Canyon Pam was contacted by the business that works closely with Kaiser in providing prosthetics. The person who runs the company not only fits the individual with the prosthetics himself, but he also has prosthetics as well. One day he came in with molds for both of Pam's legs. Within a few days, Pam was wearing artificial feet. The physical therapy technicians slowly began the process of teaching Pam how to walk again. Boy, was she ever excited! By April she was able to walk around the halls of Reche Canyon with the aid of a walker and someone following behind with an oxygen tank. Not only was she developing the strength in her legs, but she was also building up her stamina and increasing the air intake for her lungs. As an added surprise, Pam became three inches taller. By the end of April, Pam and I were able to go out to one of the patios and spend some time outside. At the same time, she remained off the vent for almost two months. We felt this could be a turning point.

One of the discharge planners wanted to set up a meeting with the staff. I had a good idea what this was going to be about. It was fairly the same process when she was at Lakeview. Everybody seemed to be optimistic in that she has shown vast improvement. We may be looking at a release date very shortly. Then came the two matters at hand. First of all, the question regarding the $7,980.00. I did not want to tell them but I had already told Pam her initial Social Security check finally came in. This covered the six months waiting period. During my last discussion with the business manager, it was made known unless we are able to handle the co-payment very shortly, he may file suit over this. I calmly told the staff to please give me at least one week and they will have their money. Because the check was solely in her name, I had Pam endorse it so that I could deposit it in her checking account through the ATM. This way we would not run into any problems with the credit union. The second matter was whether or not I had applied with Social Services for state aid. They were under the impression we were to embarrassed to apply and that is why they haven't heard from Social Services. After taking a deep breath, I told them I have been battling with them for the past year. Because of the holds the credit union places on transactions, I was unable to provide the proper documentation in time. One of the planners said they will look into the matter and get back to me.

A few days later I heard back from the discharge planner. What she had to tell me was a prime example of the state bureaucracy. The initial application went through Social Services in Orange County. This was due to the location of New Orange Hills. Reche Canyon is located in San Bernardino County! In the meantime, New Orange Hills advised Social Services in Orange County Pam is no longer a patient there. I could speed up time by going to the Social Services Department in San Bernardino County and pick up the paperwork, but it would take time to provide the necessary documentation. By this time I had the old saying going through my mind, "What we have here is failure to communicate!" This information came at the wrong time. Shortly afterwards, Pam came down with pneumonia, had to be placed back on the ventilator and was rushed to Kaiser in Riverside.

CHAPTER 11

RUNNING IN CIRCLES IS UNHEALTHY

Against her wishes, Pam was moved back to Kaiser in Riverside. She did not like it there and expressed her displeasures in no uncertain terms. I began receiving calls from the social workers expressing their concern regarding Pam's state of mind. I pointed out to them Pam's concern was to be closer to her family. At the same time, the entire staff at Lakeview is very familiar with her case. For this reason, she is requesting to be moved back to Lakeview. Transferring her by ambulance isn't a problem. The problem is if Lakeview has a room to accommodate her in I.C.U. After a few days of calls going between Riverside and Lakeview Pam was transferred back to Lakeview. Once I received the message I was sure this brought her spirits up.

I was able to visit her over the weekend. Sometimes, I would take time off during the week. Of course, she was back on the ventilator meaning she could not speak. She would remain like this for the next couple months. The major drawback was Lakeview did not have the facility or means for physical therapy for those with prosthetics. This would present a problem when it came time to transfer her back to a nursing facility. We already knew New Orange Hills did not want her back. What made matters worse was after we paid Reche Canyon the amount due, we received word they did not want Pam as well. This made it difficult because we were advised there are few skilled nursing facilities that are able to accommodate patients on a ventilator with needs for bedside dialysis. Needless to say, this brought her spirits down.

One Sunday afternoon really illustrated how this set back affected us. I was already at the I.C.U. Unfortunately, Pam was back on the vent and could not speak. I could see the hurt in her eyes fully aware she knew Reche Canyon did not want her back. Her parents arrived shortly afterwards. To my surprise all what Lucien did was pull up a chair and just stare out the window. I tried not to let it bother me since I was certain this had been taking a toll on him. This happened just as the NBA playoffs began. While making small talk with Pam, Lucien suggested that we turn the Laker game on. Pam had the controls for the television. While she was trying to locate the game, Lucien swung his chair around so that he was facing the television.

The game itself was a see saw battle. I really did not have any interest in the game. Every so often I would glance to see what the score was. As halftime approached, Lucien began moving around in his seat. He turned to me and surprisingly asked, "What's going on?" This startled me because I could see he was watching the game.

"Its halftime," I answered.

"Who's winning?" This stunned me because he was the one wanting to watch the game.

"Who is winning?" I took a deep breath and said I have to be leaving because I had work to do around the home. On the way home I'm thinking to myself, "How much longer can my in-laws hold out?"

As time went on, Pam was slowly weaned off the vent again. The same thing happened again in that at first Pam would have panic attacks. The respiratory technicians would then lower the volume without her knowing it to the point she was doing most of the breathing. I felt guilty about doing this, but we saw it as a concerted effort for her to strengthen her breathing. Eventually, the therapists were able to deflate the cuff and we had her talking again.

We were not finished with Reche Canyon. All of Pam's personal belongings, including the prosthetic feet were still out there. I drove out there to pick up the belongings that were already boxed up. Most of them I dropped off at Lakeview since we did not know when and where Pam was going to be transferred to. Pam was happy to see I was able to recover everything. One day Pam had one of the physical therapists put on her prosthetics and surprise the staff by walking out to the nurse's station with the aid of a walker and a therapist following behind with an oxygen tank. All the nurses were excited that they were taking photos depicting her walking.

It came time for another staff meeting. One of the discharge planners wanted to schedule a meeting to discuss Pam's current status and what options will be available to us. In passing, she mentioned that New Orange Hills might want to accept her back. I just gazed at her. I still was not sure whether or not the doctor at New Orange Hills heard how I ended that one particular phone conversion. At the same time I was wondering if the staff at Lakeview had a closed door discussion with the staff at New Orange Hills indicating Pam was back on life support less than forty-eight hours after they determined she was ready to be released. I went back to Pam's room advising her of this. She appeared to be more stunned than I was. We both know our options were rather slim. I told Pam I'll attend the meeting, but I will be on my best behavior, no four letter words or facsimiles thereof.

The same people were present at the meeting. It started off with one of the discharge planners thanking me for paying Reche Canyon the outstanding balance. I did not say anything knowing I did not want to piss anybody off. They went on to say this last set back really hurt Pam. The scans show her lungs have yet to heal. She has only 35% capacity using both her lungs. The prognosis did not look good and her chances of returning home are not very good as well. At the same time because she has been receiving dialysis for over a year, she may have permanent kidney damage and will need to be dialyzed for the rest of her life. Then they asked what my feelings were on this. I knew the chances of her being released this year are nonexistent. Seeing I was on the same page they were, they proceeded she was healthy enough to be transferred back to a skilled nursing facility. Reche Canyon has declined to allow Pam back there. The planner did go on to say New Orange Hills might accept her back. I sat there motionless waiting to hear more. She indicated, "Sometimes we have a bad day and might say something we don't mean to." If she is making references to my discussion with the staff doctor, then I did mean everything I said. Discussions between the two facilities were ongoing and it was just a matter of time waiting for the outcome.

I went back to Pam's room giving her a blow by blow account of the meeting. If anything, she did not mind being moved back to New Orange Hills since she was familiar with everybody there and she would be much closer to her family. The days went by and the decision had yet to be made. A few days later I heard from the discharge planner that Pam was accepted back at New Orange Hills. She was transferred back on the 18th of May. This means I had to start the process all over again with Social Services. Approximately 90% of the documents had been completed. Our main problem was canceling her IRA.

Once she was returned to New Orange Hills, it was business as usual. Each day she would have her physical therapy sessions and took part in the group activities. Most of her friends were still there, at least the ones that did not pass on. In the meantime, I was still plugging away with Social Services while trying to keep focused at work.

Some of my co-workers could see this was taking a toll on me. My quality of work had gone down so much that meetings were arranged pointing out my mistakes and asking what I was going to do to correct this. I just wanted to disappear from the face of the earth hoping this nightmare would end.

As weeks went by, Pam was showing great improvement. The therapists had her up and around while she was eventually weaned off the vent. There were days that we were able to spend time on the patio. The doctors were so impressed that Pam wanted to take a big step forward. My 50th birthday was coming up, but unfortunately it fell on a Wednesday. I would be up at our East LA office that day. I would be looking at anywhere from two to three hours in traffic just to get to New Orange Hills. Pam had discussed this with the doctors in that she would wear a canula while receiving oxygen. There was a restaurant near New Orange Hills that accommodates the handicapped. Pam wanted to go and nothing was going to stop her. Although the doctors felt she was up to it, I kept on asking her if she could do this. Again, she let it be known nothing was going to stop her.

As the big day drew closer I was more worried about taking her to the restaurant than turning fifty. The Sunday before the big date Pam gave me a list of clothes and accessories for me to bring so she could wear for the big date. As luck would have it, the day before the big date I received a call from the nurse's station. Pam came down with a severe infection and was transported to the emergency room at Orange Medical Center. Just like the previous times I rushed down there. They had been in contact with Lakeview and arrangements were made to move her back there. I was so stunned I could not speak for the rest of the day. The following day after I visited Pam, I went back home and spent the rest of the day starring at the walls.

Pam spent at least one week at Lakeview receiving I.V. solutions of antibiotics. I on the other hand was a basket case. Once she got back to New Orange Hills she was restricted on what she could do. This went on until another setback. Pam began to pass blood into the trach. Again, I received a call regarding this. It came at the most inopportune time because I just had another meeting regarding the quality of my work. I just went numb after that session. The doctors at New Orange Hills were going to try local anesthetics to see if this stops the bleeding. I couldn't take anymore and went to Urgent Care. The first thing the nurses do is take the blood pressure. The first time the nurse took the reading, a look of bewilderment came across her face and said, "This couldn't be right." She waited a couple minutes before she made another attempt. The reading came out the same, 217/175. I was a walking time bomb ready to go off any second. One of the doctors walked in and told me I should be in the hospital in no uncertain terms. I told her I was burnt out and needed time off. She was not in a position to write me off, but she immediately sent me to the psychiatric office for evaluation. I went there and met with the evaluating nurse. I told her what has been going on for the last eighteen months. She wanted me to be evaluated by a social worker, but the earliest I could get in was this coming Friday, which happened to be in two more days. I figured I could take the next couple days off. After that, it would be up to the doctor to determine the length of time I should be off. That night I called my immediate supervisor telling him I need the next couple days off. After that, it is anybody's guess how long it would be after that. Now, I have become the patient.

The following day I spent at New Orange Hills. Pam was back on the vent and could not speak. The respiratory technician was constantly in performing the suction procedure. There wasn't much in the way of mucus coming out, but they were removing large quantities of blood. Later that afternoon a call went out to the staff at Lakeview advising them of Pam's condition. They were told to keep a close monitor on her and advise me of any sudden changes. Once I returned home I called family members and friends advising them of Pam's status.

The following morning started out the same. I knew I had to leave earlier to visit Pam because of my appointment with the social worker early in the afternoon. I figured that meeting should not take long. Just be reading the notes by the evaluating nurse would be sufficient enough for me to see a specialist. The next thing I knew the phone rang. It was the nurse's station at New Orange Hills. Pam was bleeding uncontrollably and she was in the process of being transferred to the emergency room at Orange Medical Center, which happens to be just down the street from New Orange Hills. I immediately called my in-laws advising them what is going on. I then took off to the Orange Medical Center.

Around this time, Southern California was in the middle of a heat wave. It was mid morning, but the temperature was already near one hundred degrees. As I started down the road I turned on the air conditioner. I knew it would be a while, but eventually it would make the drive a bit more comfortable. This wasn't the case because hot air was pouring out while the dial was set on the maximum setting. "Great," I was thinking to myself. "What else could go wrong now that the air conditioner died?" I didn't take long to find out the answer. I went straight to the emergency room upon my arrival and asked the receptionist about the status on Pam. She called back to the emergency room and a couple minutes later told me they did not have a patient by the name of Pam. They must be mistaken! Earlier I received a call from New Orange Hills indicating she was being rushed to the Orange Medical Center. The distance is only a mile, if that. Again, she indicated they do not have a patient by the name of Pam. I got back on the phone to the nurse's station at New Orange Hills and politely asked what in the hell is going on? I was placed on hold while the nurse contacted the ambulance company. A few minutes later she came back on the line indicating they decided to move her to St. Joseph's Medical Center, which happens to be another three miles down the road. I slammed the receiver down and flew out of the waiting room.

As mentioned, St. Joseph's is another three miles down the road. This is the same location the injured players from Angel's Stadium are brought to. As I approached the medical center I could see the entrance to the emergency room. I turned down the side street I thought led to the parking lot. To my surprise there wasn't a driveway that led to the parking lot. One had to enter from the main street through a gated guard shack. I'm thinking to myself, "I'm going to pay just to see my wife during a medical emergency."

I went straight to the receptionist desk asking about Pam. She called back to the emergency room. Pam was there and the receptionist let me in. Immediately, the nurses gave me forms to complete and asked about her situation. Just like many times before, I gave a summary over the past twenty months. Once that was completed I went back to the room where

Pam was. She had a frightened look on her face. I didn't know whether or not I could say anything to calm her down. In the meantime, the staff at St. Joseph's was attempting to contact the staff at Lakeview.

A couple hours past and after looking at my watch it dawned on me I have that meeting in another hour. So far a decision had yet to be made if Pam was to be moved back to Lakeview. Most likely she will be, but I was unable to hang around. I told the nurses I had an appointment I could not reschedule in another hour. They gave me the direct phone number to the emergency room. Once I had a chance to break free I could call them for the status. I left the emergency room, paid my parking fee (the emergency room did not validate parking stubs) and drove up the freeway in the one hundred plus heat to get to my appointment.

By the time I arrived at the doctor's office, I was soaked with sweat, had yet to eat and was not in the mood to hear something to the effect, "Being upset will not make the situation better." Once I met the social worker, I apologized for my appearance and explained to her what has been going on today while I handed her copies of the paperwork I completed at St. Joseph's. After looking over the notes by the interviewing nurse and glancing over the paperwork I handed her there wasn't much for me to say why I was there. She saw to it that the doctor who saw me two days ago will indicate I need the next two days off. She immediately scheduled me to see a psychiatrist this coming Monday. The psychiatrist will determine the length of time I will need to remain off from work. I asked to borrow a phone so that I could call St. Joseph's to find out the status on Pam. Without any hesitation she handed me the phone and I proceeded to call. I was told arrangements were under way to transfer Pam back to I.C.U. at Lakeview. Once there, the staff will begin a number of tests. I left a message with my supervisor that I would not be in on Monday with the possibility of being out indefinitely.

I waited until late in the morning on Saturday before I went to Lakeview. Tests were completed last night as well as earlier in the morning. The fiberoptic laryngoscopy revealed she was bleeding from her lungs. The combination of suction and coughing caused the irritation. Those familiar with a trach would know this. The constant rubbing would cause the membranes to tear causing the bleeding. Also, every time she would cough the scar tissue would loosen and peel away causing the bleeding. It is the same process if you or I were to peel a scab. What the doctors decided was to perform a procedure by inserting a fiber optic into the lungs to find the source of bleeding. Once found, the damaged area will be cauterized immediately stopping the bleeding. Of course, she would have to be anesthetized through the entire process. Needless to say, the doctors wanted to complete this that same afternoon. I was with Pam for about an hour before the staff wheeled her downstairs to complete this. I stayed in the lobby for a couple hours. I checked with the front desk and was told they were still working on her. Knowing she would be groggy afterwards I decided to go back home.

The following Monday was my turn. I spent a session with Dr. Anjali Mangat discussing with her what has been going on for the past two years. It was easy to see why I was burnt out. She immediately authorized that I would be off for at least eight weeks. In the meantime, additional sessions were scheduled and she prescribed some medication.

Now that I had the time off, I devoted as much time I needed to deal with Social Services. All except for two items were completed: the most recent credit union monthly statement and her I.R.A. In the case of her monthly statement, we could only hope her last transaction took. In the case of her I.R.A. I attempted to use a general power of attorney just as I was using with other transactions. This was unacceptable to the bank. The bank officer checked with their legal department. A copy of the power of attorney was faxed to the legal department for review. An hour later they called back saying no and I would have to use one of their releases. The same went for access to the safety deposit box. I would have to use one of their power of attorneys. I pointed out the safety deposit box application is worded Cliff or Pam Koch. They said because of the Security Act, because my signature was not on the application at the time the safety deposit box was taken out, the only way was Pam would have to appear in person to obtain anything from the safety deposit box. I then asked to speak to the representative at the legal department. I was told the general public was not allowed to speak to their legal department. I could feel the veins bulging on my neck. Seeing I was not going to get very far I just asked for the necessary documents so that I could take them to Pam and have her sign them.

Within a few days Pam was back at New Orange Hills. At the same time I had the two documents that needed to be completed by Pam. One of them needed to be notarized. At first I thought this was going to present a problem. Once again, I got back to Marcie at Lakeview. I had an idea they are faced with this situation especially with the patients in I.C.U. I asked if she had some type of list of notaries that would be able to travel to the patient's bedside in order to notarize the necessary documents. She provided me with a list of local notaries that do travel. I was able to contact one and immediately set up an appointment. A couple days later, we met at Pam's bedside and took care of everything within a few minutes.

The following Monday I went to the bank with the necessary documents. Although the documents were printed on the bank's letterhead the documents had to be faxed to their legal department for review. They were faxed and again I had to wait for an answer. An hour later the bank representative came back with an answer the documents were unacceptable. "What do you mean they are unacceptable? You rejected the general power of attorney I initially presented saying it had to be one of your documents. Now I presented it on one of yours and now you tell me no," I shouted. It was pointed out the document to close out the I.R.A. was not signed properly. Apparently there were spaces that need her signature and she failed to do so. Also, on the power of attorney for the safety deposit box, the notary did not sign her name in the proper location. The document for the I.R.A. I could understand where she did not sign, but I pointed out not only where the notary signed, but it included her stamp. The bank officer turned back a couple pages and showed me the section asking for a witness signature. I happened to sign it since I was the witness. According to the bank officer, the notary should have signed there. We were nearing the due date for the documents for Social Services. The officer gave me fresh copies because we had to start all over.

I got back to the notary so we could set up another meeting. Because of her busy schedule we had to wait until the end of the week. She was rather surprised I called her back, but something like this by the bank didn't surprise her. Again, we obtained the necessary signed and notarized documents. The following Monday I was at the bank early so we could get this resolved. Again, I had to wait for final approval from the legal department. The bank officer got back to me saying the power of attorney was acceptable. However, the application for the I.R.A. still was not signed properly. I knew my face was turning red because I was biting hard on my back molars. They were able to let me back to the safety deposit box, but Pam would still need to complete another application for the I.R.A.

I went back to New Orange Hills and by that time Pam could see I was ready to explode. We just sat there trying to figure out what next since we had a little more than two weeks for the documents to be in. I came up with the idea that we will have an ambulance take her from the nursing facility and transport her to the bank. We can wheel her in on a stretcher with a respiratory therapist present and take care of everything once and for all. At first she thought I was joking, but I was very serious about this. I was to check this out the following day, but as luck would have it, Pam developed another infection and was bleeding again. She was transferred back to Lakeview for the same treatments. I remembered sitting in the lobby staring off into space while the doctors were attempting to cauterize the bleeding from her lungs. Dr. Sivjee happened to walk by and asked if Pam was back. I just nodded my head yes. He asked if it was for the same thing and again I just nodded my head yes without saying a word.

I eventually went back to the bank on my best behavior. I sat down with the bank officer and proceeded to explain the importance of finishing this one document because of the deadline. I described in great detail Pam's current physical condition and the fact she's back in I.C.U. I suggested since an attempt had failed twice, if she could bring the application in person. This would resolve this matter once and for all. After giving it some thought, she indicated yes, but she would have to check with the branch manager. She was gone for the day, but if I check back tomorrow I would have an answer. The following day I called and sure enough it was a go. A couples days later both bank representatives were out and showed Pam where to sign. I went to the nurse's station and had them make a photocopy. I then showed the discharge planner that this was the final document and it will be off in the mail before the end of the day. That afternoon I went home under the impression that everything is finally falling into place. Little did I know lightning was about to strike for a second time.

CHAPTER 12

THE NIGHTMARE WORSENS

September was about to end and I felt confident it would be a matter of time before everything was squared away with Social Services, or so I thought. Wednesday the 29th of September I ran into Marcie before I got to Pam's room. She asked, "Have you submitted the paperwork yet?"

"Yes, as a matter of fact," I answered. "In fact I showed one of your co-workers the final document that Social Services needed and it has long since been mailed out." It seemed rather odd she would ask this, because she knew I was on top of everything that was going on behind the scenes. "It is possible they may want to release Pam soon," she indicated. That's fine, but what also seemed rather odd was I was receiving calls from New Orange Hills asking if I submitted the paperwork yet. We knew it was a matter of time for Social Services to give the okay. Marcie said she would check on this before the end of today because beginning tomorrow she would be leaving on a four day weekend.

Nothing exciting occurred during my visit. Pam was scheduled for dialysis, but unfortunately they started just before lunch. This meant she would have a late lunch or skip it altogether. I was more worried about Marcie contacting Social Services. I did not want Pam to know what was going on. Just as I was leaving Marcie saw me and pulled me to the side. No word so far from Social Services, but not to worry. She went on to say in the event Pam is to be released, we can ask for an arbitration hearing. Pam's case would be sent to a panel of doctors for review. It usually takes a couple days before a decision is made. They can hold off and wait until

Friday before submitting the paperwork and the earliest a decision would be made will not be until Tuesday. It wasn't exactly what I wanted to hear, but I'll take it.

The following day as I walked by the nurse's station one of them told me the discharge planers wanted to meet with me in Pam's room. I had an uneasy feeling this was about to get nasty. I told Pam about the meeting and the fact I didn't have any idea what this was going to be about. As the meeting started I noticed it was rather odd that there were two discharge planners along with one of the social workers and one of the nurses happened to be in the room. The meeting started out by one of the planners asking me if I ever signed the documents and submitted them to Social Services. I answered yes and as a matter of fact the last document that we had the most difficult time with was shown to one of her co-workers before it was mailed out. The next question was did I receive a return receipt? I told her no because everything was mailed to a PO Box and one can't send a registered letter with return receipt to a PO Box. "Well then, do you have copies of all the signed documents and other items sent to Social Services," she asked? I told her no because all the documents provided were forms that were triplicate with instructions to return all the pages. The remainder was front and back copies of bank statements along with transactions. If I knew better it was just as if I was being scolded for not doing anything of what she asked. The planner went on to say Pam is ready to be released today and she needs to be moved. I then asked if they heard from Social Services. That was answered with a resounding no. I then inquired about New Orange Hills. She told me, "New Orange Hills will not accept her back until they have documentation showing she has been accepted by Social Services."

As mentioned earlier, this was the first meeting with Pam present. Seeing and hearing what was going on made Pam very upset. Needless to say, I was becoming agitated as well. I told them that I was not going to sign any releases authorizing Pam to be moved because we don't have anywhere to go. The other planner asked something to the effect of allowing her to go home. "No way," I shouted. She was still on the vent, she will need constant monitoring plus I still had fresh memories of what happened two months ago. Pam was crying uncontrollably while the nurse was trying to calm her down. I then muttered something out loud that later on came back to haunt me, "I can understand why people go postal." For a few seconds nobody said a word. I finally asked about Marcie's suggestion of waiting until

Friday to ask for an arbitration hearing. It was as if I caught them off guard. They said this could be done, but in the event the decision goes against us, I might be liable for her stay in I.C.U. as well as all medications. That was a chance I had to take. Hopefully, by that time we should have some word from Social Services. I spent the rest of the afternoon attempting to calm Pam down.

I left that afternoon knowing that Pam should be there at least through Tuesday as Marcie indicated. Once I got home I must have collapsed because a couple hours later the phone woke me up. It was Doris and she was frantic. She was screaming, "Pam is very upset, they want to move her now and the staff is upset you won't sign the paperwork." I thought it was one of my nightmares, but no this was the real thing. I told Doris everything was taken care of earlier today and it is a matter of waiting for the arbitration board or Social Services before our next move. It was as if she didn't hear me. She kept on repeating herself. I finally told her to have one of the nurse's get on the phone. So I can find out what is going on. For a few minutes I could hear Doris talking in the background but I could not fully hear the discussion. A few minutes later she came back on the line telling me the nurses refuse to speak to me and that I had to go down there in person to obtain information. I slammed the receiver down, grabbed the car keys and sped off back to Lakeview.

Once I got to the lobby, Lucien happened to be there telling me they are going to move her and they want me to sign the paperwork. I told him they are not going to move her. I have asked for an arbitration hearing that would buy us some time until Tuesday. Hopefully, by that time we should hear from Social Services. The only paperwork I could think of was that for Social Services that has long been sent or the discharge papers. He goes on to say they can't move her until I sign the paperwork. I told him I'm not going to authorize her discharge. She is still on the vent, New Orange Hills will not take her back until we hear from Social Services and the only place we can move her to would be home. I do not know how to fully operate the vent as a respiratory tech would. She would need constant monitoring. If not, we may have a repeat performance just as we did two months ago. Either that or she will not survive. It was as if he did not hear one word I just told him.

"Go ahead and move her back home," he said.

"Fine, if I move her back home and she doesn't survive, are you willing to help me with the funeral expenses," I shouted back.

"I don't know," is all he said. By this time we were already up on the I.C.U. floor and I'm sure everybody up there heard us. As I was walking towards Pam's room, Doris was in the hallway just as frantic as she was when I spoke to her on the phone. I went to the nurse's station asking if there is anybody there to find out what is going on? Her nurse for the day told me all of the discharge planners have left for the day. The only thing she could do was to locate the evening discharge planner. I went into Pam's room attempting to calm her down. At the same time I was asking, "What the hell is going on here?" Doris kept on repeating herself saying they are going to move her. Lucien poked his head in the room say something to the effect it is time to go and he is leaving for the car. Doris did not want to leave until this matter was resolved.

While waiting for the evening discharge planner I sat there looking as if I was ready to explode. This made Pam even more anxious. While this was happening, I noticed two security officers standing just outside the door to Pam's room. Someone felt I was about to go postal and contacted security. I stood there with my arms folded trying to calm down before something happens and I make the late evening news.

Finally, the evening discharge planner came in. While stopping short of going ballistic I was pouring out my frustrations. I went on to say we don't have a place to move Pam and bringing her home may prove fatal. The discharge planner was going over the records and said, "Pam is not going to be moved." I stood there stunned. "Then why all of this commotion of her being moved this evening?" Nobody told her about this, but the records indicate it is a matter of waiting for the arbitration hearing. Until then, Pam will remain there. I could see Pam sunk back into her pillow looking relived. I went back to the nurse's station apologizing for being such a jerk. To this day, nobody would say why or how my in-laws were told that Pam was to be moved.

Later that evening, I received a call from Eileen wanting to know what is going on and why I will not sign the paperwork. Apparently, her father called her not knowing everything is under control. The only paperwork I could think of was the discharge papers for Pam. It would be a cold day in you know where before I allow her to be moved unless it was back to New Orange Hills. Still, nobody told me how such information was passed on to my in-laws.

The following day was business as usual. I kept a low profile while visiting Pam. I still had an uneasy feeling things are not going right and something was about to happen. All during this time, none of the planners came to the room. That was fine with me because I did not want a repeat performance of last night. The staff might be thinking all of this undue stress has already taken its toll and I'm ready to snap my cap. The truth is I was surprised I haven't flipped out yet. Little did I know my faith and integrity was about to be tested again that same Friday night.

It was already 6:00 P.M. when the phone rang. It was rather questionable the timing of this call and the way it started had me worried. It was one of the discharge planners at Lakeview. She began by saying, "This is the first time we ever had this happen! Apparently the board had plenty of time and was able to review your case. I'm sorry to say the decision went against you. You will need to make arrangements to have Pam moved."

"What do you mean," I shouted back.

"I'm sorry the decision came in at this time, but arrangements will need to be completed to move Pam," she told me.

"What if you were able to arrange to have Pam moved to New Orange Hills?"

"Because Social Services has yet to make a decision, New Orange Hills will not accept her unless you provide a cashier's check for $24,000.00 to cover her first two months."

"Where in the hell am I going to obtain a cashier's check after 6.00 P.M. on a Friday?"

"I'm sorry for the timing, but arrangements will need to be made to move Pam."

I have never felt so alone. My heart was pounding in my head and I was a nervous wreck. I went as far as calling the afterhour's line for the psychiatry department. After giving them my story of woe, I was told there was nothing they could do. If I still had nervous feelings, I always could go to urgent care. Just great, the arbitration board made a rare same day decision, Lakeview wants me to move Pam in spite of what happened two months ago, we are still waiting for Social Services and their decision, because of that New Orange Hills wants a $24,000.00 deposit and if I still feel nervous I'm to go to urgent care and probably will be medicated. I'm beginning to believe God is punishing me for a past sin.

It has been almost two years since this nightmare began. Now, we are playing bureaucracy ping-pong and I'm losing! Anybody by now would have thrown in the towel and walked away. I can see in Pam's face her desire to overcome this. If anything, she wants to come back home where she belongs. Each set back has taken its toll but she is determined. In the mean time, I'm darn near killing myself trying to keep Pam alive. I took the vow to support my wife in sickness and in health, but I'm beginning to question my faith. It is one thing the human psyche craves immediate gratification. It is a different matter when a loved one has come back from the brink of death a few times and the powers to be are more concerned where and when the money is coming in. Only a few family members and outside friends have been aware of what has been going on since day one. Now I have my back to the wall, the hospital wants her out, the nursing facility wants $24,000.00 in a cashier's check on a Friday night and everybody is telling me sorry we can't help you, but we will keep you in our prayers. I'm very seriously considering doing a disappearing act and cover my tracks so I could not be located. Pam then would become ward of the state. The chances are she would be moved to a county hospital, at which time it could be her death sentence. Needless to say, I did not get very much sleep for the rest of the weekend.

The following morning began with a phone call from one of the discharge planners. Again, they wanted to know if arrangements have been made to move Pam. I told her no at which time it was followed by her asking why. I pointed out she is still on the vent which means I would have to locate an ambulance company that would be able to accommodate a vent patient. At the same time, since I do not have $24,000.00 I would have to locate a nursing facility that would not only be able to but not limited to tend to a vent patient, but also will need to wait for Social Services to make their decision. She clearly understood what I was saying and did not have a reply. She did indicate I might be liable for her stay in I.C.U. I told her, "That is a chance I have to take."

The next two days I kept a low profile while visiting Pam, who very upset not knowing what the future had in store for her. She has come so far and is determined to beat this, but the odds are beginning to say otherwise. Her entire future remains in the balance pending Social Services decision. I feel like a reformed alcoholic taking it one day at a time.

Monday morning I dragged myself back to Lakeview. The lack of sleep was taking its toll, but I had to be near Pam's side to keep her spirits up. Aside for the nurses, nobody came into her room. Lunchtime came around and I decided to go out and get a bite to eat. Just before I entered the elevator one of the financial planners from the business office saw me. "She has been accepted," she said. I thought I was becoming delirious and hearing things, but I heard her correctly, "She has been accepted."

"As of now," I asked? "Yes, as of now."

"Did the decision just come in," I asked?

"No, the decision was made back on Friday!"

The next few seconds seemed to last an eternity. I did not know whether or not to bounce off the walls yelling "Yippee" or start saying everything imaginable with references to family ancestry, religion and biology. She went on to say the authorization came in on Friday and was placed on Marcie's desk. Because she took off on a four day weekend her office was locked and nobody knew about it. All what I need to do was get the co-payment to New Orange Hills and the arrangements will be made to move Pam. I got back to Her room to let her know what just happened. I could see the sigh of relief on her face.

I flew home to obtain the necessary amount for the co-payment. I then took off for New Orange Hills handing Stacey, the business manager, the co-payment. She indicated that most likely Pam should be moved there by this evening. I went back to Lakeview to see Pam. Just as I entered the elevator to go up to I.C.U. Marcie happened to be there. Her exact words were, "Hi, or are you still talking to us?"

"I don't know," was my answer. Unfortunately, it was the last time I either saw Marcie or talked to her.

I got to Pam's room assuring her everything is now under control. She knew how exhausted I was and wanted me to go home and just rest. It was a few days later Pam told me only one of the discharge planners came to her room and apologized for what happened. I never did hear an apology from any of the planners.

CHAPTER 13

SECOND TOUR OF DUTY

Pam was finally ready to begin her second tour of duty at New Orange Hills. The major difference was her stay was financed by state funds. Also, she was responsible for her own medication. New Orange Hills did not have a pharmacy, but carried the essentials. Because of her condition, Pam needed all sorts of medications. This meant I would have to purchase all her meds ahead of time while they were stored at the nurse's station. I would ask the nurses to warn me ahead of time when her meds were running low. A majority of the time, this was not the case. I would come home from work and play the recorder. There would be one of the nurses leaving a message Pam ran out of a certain med and I had to pick it up immediately. Usually, this was a message left early in the morning. I rarely got home before 6:00 P.M. This worried Pam because after my long day I would have to stop by long after visiting hours. This was how I celebrated one of my birthdays.

Pam had finally settled in and was back on her same routine. She was able to mingle with her friends and take in visitors. One especially used to brighten up her day. Margaret, who goes by Mac, who used to be a neighbor, would visit her, but would bring some goodies. Sometimes she would bring a cheeseburger loaded with the works from the nearest In-N-Out stand. I'm sure this was one hundred times better than the hospital food. Either that or some type of caffeine laced concoction from the local Starbuck's that was off limits in a hospital setting. Fr. Andrew would get into the act sometimes. There was a nearby hotdog stand he would stop off at. That too was usually something with the works. Pam would inhale a couple of those. Once a week her parents would bring sushi. It wasn't long before I jumped on the bandwagon. I would stop off at a nearby store that specializes in Mexican food. There was a counter where one could place orders for certain Mexican dishes. It was some of the best authentic homemade Mexican food around. We were determined to build her strength up one way or another.

I still would take some time off spending the day with Pam. If she felt up to it I would bring her lunch from one of the local fast food locations. There were days she didn't feel well and we just sat in her room. Each bed had a hook up for a small TV. Most of the time we would watch whatever was on daytime TV. We could not get involved in the soaps. It seems each one of them had a similar plot. If you missed watching a program for a few weeks and pick it up later, you really did not miss much. That is why we always watched Divorce Court. Nobody on the face of the earth could come up with a storyline that some of those couples came up with. It was better than watching some of the sitcoms. I always thought Judge Maybelline had nerves of steel sitting through some of those episodes. I would have to have a bottle stashed away in a drawer and take a belt or two depending on what kind of couple was on.

Things were running smoothly by this time, or so I though. It wasn't until the weekend before Thanksgiving that lightening struck again. That Saturday there was to be a get together at my father's place later in the day. I figured I could swing by to visit Pam later than normal before I went to my father's. I decided to call the nurse's station to see how she was doing. Her nurse came on the line saying, "She had an accident and fell. She is doing okay at this time." I knew something was wrong because the nurses could not give out any information at the time. The reason for my concern was Pam had lost so much weight her bones from her extremities were bulging out. Any fall on her hip could be a disaster.

I got to New Orange Hills and immediately saw Pam was in great pain. Again, they were giving her morphine, but the medication would wear off soon afterwards. That morning she was not wearing her prosthetics and had to go to the bathroom. One of the nurses placed her on the bedside commode, but left her there still wrapped in her hospital gown. Without the use of her left hand, she tried to lift herself up so that the gown could be removed without making a mess. As luck would have it, Pam lost her balance falling to the floor on her right hip. The scary part of this was she was on the vent and could not call out for help. She does not know how long she was on the floor, but it must of seemed an eternity before one of the nurses came into her room and found her on the floor. A call did go out to the doctors, but the staff was told just to keep her under observation.

I wanted to stay by her bedside, but she wanted me to go to my father's place. When I got there I told everybody what happened. The rest of the evening I was not in a talkative mood. I told the nurses to contact me if anything came up. Later on, I did receive a call indicating that evening they were to transfer her to Lakeview.

The next morning I called Lakeview. X-Rays revealed not only did she fracture her pelvis, but the right femur was fractured as well. That Sunday she was operated on placing staples in her pelvis and a rod to hold the femur in place. I don't think I said one word while in the waiting room. By now I am questioning my faith asking how can God do this if He knows everything about each one of us. This isn't the same God I was raised to know and love. Yet again, there is a purpose for everything, so it has been said. I began to re-examine my life and wondered what sin I committed to deserve such a fate. At the same time I'm wondering how much more trauma can she take before her body shuts down. For once in my life I was alone without any answers to my questions.

The next couple days Pam remained at Lakeview. The doctors kept her under observation while she remained on a morphine drip. Wednesday, the day before Thanksgiving, she was moved back to New Orange Hills. The doctor's orders were for her to remain in bed. The physical therapists would come in and help her move around so that she didn't develop any bedsores. Thanksgiving Day we spent watching the Macy's Parade and watched some football. Again, food services had a buffet free to the family members and patients who were able to eat that type of food. Because Pam had to remain in bed, we had our own celebration in her room. Her parents stopped by for a visit before going to Eileen's for dinner. This pretty much was the same procedure through the holidays. Both Christmas and New Year's were rather low keyed.

Nothing exciting happened during the early months of 2005. Pam was being weaned off the vent again and on recovery to begin walking again. Around the end of March beginning of April, Pam's thought processes were hard at work. This coming May 31st would have been our twenty-fifth wedding anniversary. We knew the chances were going to be slim next to none that she would be released. She wanted to reserve the family room and have a celebration. She wanted to have Fr. Andrew officiate in renewing our vowels. She wanted to have our nephew, Grant, play the piano and her parents could have it catered. It sounded fine, but over the past couple years I have been a bit hesitant in scheduling something in the future based on Pam's track record. She was so set in having this to the point Eileen and her parents were in the planning stages. Fr. Andrew was busy adjusting his schedule to be free at that time. Eileen was working hard on the food preparations and Grant could not wait to show off how good of a piano player he has become. I, on the other hand, had an uneasy feeling something was going to happen. I kept on asking Pam if she would be up to it. Of course, in her own way she wanted to.

The days were going by and Pam was getting more excited as we closed in on the end of May. Pam was strong enough that we spent an hour or two on the patio. Everybody saw this as a great sign that she was getting better. I was afraid that some nitwit would be out there with a cold coughing their germs all over and thus putting Pam back at Lakeview. Little did I know how close I came to the truth.

It was a couple days before the big day and everything was falling into place. Again, not only did Pam develop a cough, but she was bleeding into the trach. I knew for sure our planned celebration was not to be. Everybody in the family reassured me not to worry and everything will be fine. How could everything be fine when we rarely got a lucky break? That came to a crashing stop one week before the party, Pam had to be rushed back to Lakeview. This time her status was more serious. Not only did she have pneumonia, but she had a urinary infection and she was still bleeding into the trach. Her infection was so bad she was barely conscious. She was like that for a few days when she went into another coma.

The big day came and I did something that I now regretted, I could not bring myself to go to the hospital. I was probably the saddest person to celebrate their twenty-fifth wedding anniversary. The entire day I could not concentrate let alone get anything accomplished. From what I was told, Pam was barely conscious that day. By now I felt our future together was not to be.

While this was going on another symptom began to rear its ugly head. Her hands, arms and legs began to turn blue and were cold to the touch. She also had a bleeding episode that one night the pulmonary doctors had to rush her down to surgery. One of them wanted to cut into her chest and remove the damage that was causing this problem. Because of her condition this would have been fatal for her. They decided to cauterize the source of the bleeding. Again, this time it worked. Shortly afterwards, my in-laws and Eileen were at the hospital. The doctors in their own way came out to say the prognosis is not good. Eileen had a chance to read the latest medical report. The end of it read, "I don't expect her to survive much longer, but she has nine lives like a cat."

Later that evening I received a call from Eileen. I could tell by the tone in her voice she did not have good news. She described to me the latest medical report placing emphasis on the final sentence. She then recommended that the both of us begin to look for a casket while we won't be as traumatized by her passing. At first I could not say anything. I knew Pam was living on borrowed time and sooner or later her luck will run out. It is a matter of when it will happen. We agreed within the next week we will spend the day looking for a casket.

After I hung up, I just broke down. All of this was constantly hitting me from all angles without any relief for this mental anguish. I went ahead and called my childhood friend, Chuck, who happened to live in Minnesota. Both he and his wife, Julie Ann knew what was happening and I constantly kept them posted. I knew he was probably in bed, but I was desperate to speak and listen to a friendly voice. He could tell I seemed to be walking on the edge. I poured out my entire soul, something I needed to do. I knew some day I will need a favor or two and this happened to be the one time.

My next few visits were very somber. I could only pull up a chair alongside her bed and just hold her hand. I couldn't say anything but just stare at her. One day, my father and his friend, Fran, stopped by for a visit. They could see in my face the agony I was going through and couldn't do anything for it. A few weeks later Fran told me how upset she was seeing Pam there that once she got back home she said a rosary.

While I was alone, Dr. Chan happened to walk by. He gave me the most up to date information regarding her condition. He then said something I kept to myself and haunted me every day. He said, "Pam's heart has become so weak if she needed to be resuscitated, let along having the staff call Code Blue the chances she will not survive."

If there ever was a time we needed a miracle, this was it.

All of this was happening at the same time the Teri Schivao case was going on in Florida. For those who don't recall, this was the situation Teri was comatose for years and her husband wanted to stop feeding her. Her parents on the other hand had different ideas expecting complete recovery. Everybody from Governor Jeb Bush to the Florida State Supreme Court got involved. Pam may not have been sick that long, but I had a good idea what Mr. Schivao was going through. I wanted to speak to him, but I'm sure he was hounded by the media all day long. We were lucky in that Pam's condition did not get that bad, but Pam was a heartbeat away from the inevitable.

To make matters worse, Pam developed a bedsore on her back. Because the nurses did not think she was going to survive she was not moved while all of this was going on. It was an open wound that had to be carefully guarded. Keeping in mind Pam was very thin from all of this to the point if the wound became infected and should spread to her spine, it would prove fatal. We were running out of option not to mention we were running out of time.

As time went on her white cell count began to slowly decrease. This meant her infection(s) were slowly on their way out. Every day the nurses would change the dressing over the bedsore while applying ointment to help the healing process. The doctors already had her on an air mattress to relieve the pressure on the bedsore. At times she appeared to be uncomfortable, but that was a good sign in that she was aware of her surroundings. Although she could not talk, shortly afterwards she was able to write questions and answers. Of course, she did not remember anything that happened. That was the least of our worries. As a matter of fact, we did not have to pick out a casket.

One day while we were alone I had to confront her with the inevitable. Remembering what Dr. `Chan told me I looked her straight in the eye and said, "You were lucky and dodged another bullet. The next time your luck may run out. I need to know now if anything happens do you or do you not want a funeral?" A few seconds went by before she weakly shook her head yes.

It was the middle of July the doctors had her moved back to New Orange Hills. The day she was to be moved, I took her belongings back there. Because she was gone for so long, another patient was in her bed. Because the staff did not know what room she would be in, I left the belongings at the nurse's station. I went to the family room, pulled up a chair and decided to take a break. Nobody saw me walk in but the conversations I could overhear were about Pam. Nobody knew how she was doing let alone if she was coming back. You should have seen the shock on their faces when they saw me and I told them she should be back within the next couple hours. I was already gone when the paramedics wheeled her back in. I was told the staff gathered around giving her a standing ovation. I probably would of lost it if I was there.

CHAPTER 14

LAST CALL

Pam began her third attempt at rehabilitation and it was business as usual. This time she had strict orders to remain on the vent and she could not be moved from her bed. The nurses and therapists could have her change positions to relieve the pressure from the bedsore, not to mention avoid another one. The staff was pleased how the bedsore was healing. In the meantime, friends and family brought in goodies from the outside world. This pretty much kept her spirits up in spite of the circumstances. This was basically the routine for the next three months.

Just before Thanksgiving, she was finally allowed to start weaning off the vent and she was able to leave her bed. Surprisingly, it did not take long for her to begin using her prosthetic legs and getting around while using a walker. Because her energy levels were low most of the time she got around in a wheel-chair. After what happened five months ago, everybody felt Pam was going in the right direction.

Thanksgiving Day finally came but it was quite different. Instead of being bedridden I was able to wheel her to the family room for the day's festivities. Again, New Orange Hills had a buffet for the patients who were able to participate and their family members. After watching the Macy's Thanksgiving Day Parade I wheeled her into the family room so that we could celebrate our own Thanksgiving Dinner. Surprisingly, Pam was able to eat her fair share of turkey and all the trimmings. All during this time David, one of the respiratory therapists, had a hand held camcorder recording everybody's thoughts for the day. He introduced Pam as a special person and a true miracle just to be with us. Pam gave thanks to all the people that have tended to her helping her on the road to recovery. I was thankful for the doctors, nurses, staff members and all the patients and friends that have been involved in helping Pam. This was the last recorded live video image of Pam.

As Christmas neared, Pam received an early surprise. Fr. Andrew and his congregation donated funds to purchase a portable DVD player. I was not there when she received it, but one could see the excitement in her eyes as she showed me what she received. Her friend Mac and I proceeded to bring her DVDS of her favorite movies and TV shows. She had a fairly good size library by the time Christmas rolled around.

The staff had brought in miniature Christmas Trees for the patients to decorate their own way. I went one step further. Through a mail order catalog I purchased a Christmas Tree decorated with Boston terriers all over. I know how much she missed our own Boston terrier, but with this and an 8X10 snapshot of our Boston would add to the atmosphere. At this rate the staff had to bring in extra tables to accommodate her new toys.

One thing she really wanted was a laptop. She told everybody she wanted to tell all what happened to her. The radio station she listened to had a gift give away. Each hour the DJ would take a call from one of the listeners, who would then ask for a special gift for that one unfortunate friend. The problem was one had to call a toll free number and leave a message on a recorder. As one would guess that line was constantly busy. Pam was able to get through and left a message. She went on to say how close she was to death and how she wanted to write about her experiences. We will never know whether or not somebody heard her request. At the same time I could not believe a person could suffer so much and was able to talk about it.

On Christmas Eve, Santa's little helpers were hard at work. When Pam woke up the following morning, she found a laptop by her side. At first she thought either her parents or myself brought it in. She found out this wasn't the case since it was hours before we stopped by. It turned out Bill, one of the technicians who performed her kidney dialysis, was the little elf. Bill's wife was in a business where she was constantly receiving new laptops. Instead of throwing this one away, Bill decided to give it to Pam. She was very excited and wanted to begin her writings immediately. She made me promise to fill in the blanks. This meant I was to write about what happened behind the scenes as well as everything that happened while she was unconscious. I let her know some might be hurt as to what happened.

Christmas 2005 finally arrived. I spent just about the entire day with Pam. Her parents stopped by for a little while before going on to Eileen's. The staff members would stop by giving us their best wishes as well as the other patients and their families. Everybody was caught up in the Christmas spirit. I'm glad they were because it would be our last Christmas together.

As the New Year began everybody was upbeat as to how Pam was coming along. Our monthly meeting with the staff began with the doctors possibly considering on removing the trach. The nursing staff wanted us to take her rehab one step further. Weather permitting we would be able to start going outside the facility. While hooked up to an oxygen tank, I would be able to wheel her around the sidewalk in front of New Orange Hills. If Pam really felt up to it, I would be able to take her to the nearest video store so she could select a movie or a game. Her parents wanted to go one step further in taking Pam to one of the Sunday Services at their church. Every Sunday her parents would tell the congregation and keep them posted on her condition. She was almost like a celebrity in their eyes and everybody wanted to see her. I like the idea, but the mornings were fairly cold by California's standards. I suggested we should wait until it gets warmer because it won't take much for her catch pneumonia placing her back at Lakeview. Her parents agreed with me and we decided to wait until it warms up before we take her to a Sunday Service. Little did I know this was not to be.

Prior to all of this, Pam had let us know what her next project was to be. She wanted to take part in the L.A. Marathon. David, one of the respiratory therapists competed in the previous year's race. Rich also was a veteran of the L.A. Marathon, not to mention the Boston Marathon. It really was not a far-fetched idea. Each year there is a handicapped division competing in their wheelchairs or whatever devices that gets them around the course. The doctors and staff were all for it. Rich was to contact a company on the east coast that specializes in wheelchairs or other mechanisms for the handicapped. The day of the race, Rich would push Pam along the course. I would have to be staked out at various locations on the course with fresh oxygen tanks. The plan was to push Pam through the entire race. With about ten yards from the finish, Pam was to get out of the chair and walk across the finish line. We thought for sure we had a page one feature story for all the local newspapers. At the same time, I told her not to get any ideas about New York.

Pam spent her days divided between the physical therapy and working on her story. Each day she appeared to be getting stronger with the main goal of making it to the L.A. Marathon. In spite of her condition, she was able to spend extended periods out on the patio. Saturday February 25th both Pam and I spent on the patio talking. She was so excited the race was less than a month away and she really wanted to compete in it. I just wanted her to remain healthy through that time period so that it would be another step closer she would be able to come home. It wasn't too long ago Eileen and myself were about to start planning a funeral when Pam pulled through another setback. I still had the feeling we were on borrowed time, but just as the doctor said, "She is a cat with nine lives."

The following day we received a dose of reality. As I entered her room I noticed she was back on the vent. The night before she began coughing again with some bleeding. The staff did not waste any time and placed her back on the vent. She was fairly stable but she did have that cough. She didn't appear to be too alarmed, but I could see she was bothered. I felt she was going to have a relapse and all the work up to this moment would be wasted. All afternoon I tried to make small talk with her, but I was too upset. As I left for the day I remember telling her something to make her smile. As I left I said, "No more bugs or we will have to call you cootie."

Monday, February 27 there wasn't any change. She remained stable for her condition while the nurses kept a close eye on her.

Tuesday, February 28, after finishing diner I suddenly had an urge to call to see how she was doing. The receptionist had problems transferring me back to the nurse's station. Once I was connected I found out why. Pam was having difficulties and they went in the process of calling the paramedics. She was going to be moved to Orange Medical Center, which was approximately one mile from New Orange Hills. In a matter of seconds I ran up the stairs, grabbed my wallet and keys and was out the door on my way to Orange Medical Center. She was already in the emergency room when I arrived. They could not let me back there yet because they were working on her. During that wait, both Pam's parents and eventually Rich stopped by. Eileen stayed home with the boys. It was a whole hour before I was allowed to go back to see Pam. Again, she was hooked up to every type of machine imaginable. The attending physician came by telling me not only is she having problems breathing, but her heart rate was unstable. Their main concern was to stabilize her. In the meantime, they would contact Lakeview to see if she could be transferred. The doctor finished by saying the prognosis was not good. I spent a fairly good portion of the evening by her bedside. The emergency crew was able to stabilize her and she was moved back to Lakeview. When I left it must have been just before dawn.

I forced myself to get up early that morning. I called work telling them what happened last night. I would not be coming in that day and most likely the following day as well. Pam had already been moved back to Lakeview. I tried to get there as early as possible. I first stopped at the nurse's station to check her status. She was somewhat stable for her condition, but still had the irregular heart beat. The doctors wanted to stabilize it before conducting any tests. She was scheduled for dialysis later that morning. I just remained at her bedside except for going out to get some lunch. Again, she could see the anguish in my eyes. It was very difficult to speak to her plus she was unable to speak because of being on the vent.

Her dialysis session went smoothly without any problems. Again, the technician was able to remove the toxins that continue to build up in her body. Just as the technician was finishing up, I noticed something I have not seen in a long time. Pam began to get a panic attack. I don't know whether or not she had her medications earlier, but even on the vent her breathing became irregular. I tried to calm her down by speaking softly telling her to breathe slowly and everything will be fine. Just as she was calming down I noticed something never seen before. One of the nurses wheeled the crash cart up to the entrance of her room. I stood there stunned for what seemed as a long time. Not wanting to show I was upset of what was going on I kept on telling her everything will be okay. About an hour later, I decided to leave. After each dialysis session she was tired. Just as I was leaving one of the nurses brought in a snack. The nurse stood by her bedside answering questions while Pam was writing questions on a piece of paper. Neither one of them saw I was standing at the doorway but I just stood there staring at Pam wondering how many more setbacks her body can handle. I would have my answer in less than twenty-four hours.

Thursday, March 2, 2006, the day started out as usual. I was able to get some sleep after what happened a couple days ago. Pam wanted me to bring in some of her belongings from New Orange Hills. I stopped off loading up a bag or two with some of her belongings to hold her over while at Lakeview. It took longer than usual because I could not find everything she wanted. I figured I better hurry up or she will get excited thinking something might have happened to me.

I got there to Lakeview and rode the elevator up to the seventh floor. No sooner I stepped out onto the floor, I was pulled aside by one of the nurses. She told me, "Pam has been having breathing difficulties that we had to resuscitate her. It doesn't look good." She led me through the doors leading to the unit. As I'm entering I can hear on the intercom, "Code Blue seventh floor . . . . Code Blue seventh floor!" As I approached her room I'm thinking this can't be happening. I could see the crash cart in her room as she was surrounded by doctors and nurses. Dr. Chan greeted me at the entrance. He told me, "Pam has been having breathing difficulties. We have resuscitated her three times already. It is very possible she may have brain damage. Your will need to make a decision."

An icy tingle went down my spine. About the same time the last thirty years flashed before me. "This can't be happening." I'm thinking to myself. Unfortunately, this was the real thing. I'm watching the doctors and nurses tend to her while she was lying there probably unconscious with brain damage while her body was involuntary gasping for the precious oxygen needed to sustain life. At that moment, Rev. Richard Lewis, the hospital's chaplain walked into the room. Rev. Lewis got to know Pam during her stays at Lakeview. She used to have long and emotional discussions about her condition. Now, she might be breathing her last. He placed his arm around me saying, "Let's go to another room. I was lead to one of the conference rooms where we had many meetings with the staff. I sat there unable to speak due to the enormity of the situation. I knew nobody was in a position to help me, let alone give me the magic answer. Rev. Lewis went on to say, "She lead a great battle against her sickness." Having him speak in the past tense seemed to seal her fate. All what I was thinking to myself was all the clichés one hears about imminent death. Now, I'm faced with the real thing. After collecting my thoughts, we went back to her room.

As we entered the room, one of the nurses said, "We had to resuscitate her again."

Her body was still involuntary gasping for a breath of oxygen. I looked at the figures on the crash cart. Her heart rate was decreasing with each heartbeat. I stared at the clock and it was 12:00 P.M. I turned back towards her placing my hand on her shoulder and whispered, "I loved you and I always will." I then turned to Dr. Chan whispering loud enough, "Let her go."

Rev. Lewis and I went back to the conference room. Again, I just sat there in silence. Two minutes later Dr. Chan walked in saying, "She just passed away." For the next ten minutes, all of the frustrations that had built up over the past three years came flowing out. I asked Dr. Chan to remove the trach and all the tubes before her parents get here.

After regaining my composure, I had the difficult task to tell the world Pam is gone. I first called Pam's mother. She answered the phone sounding upbeat and glad to hear from me. I tried to tell her what happened. My voice broke and she could not hear me. I took a deep breath, let it out and said, "Pam is gone."

"What," she screamed over the line.

"Pam is gone," I said in a somber tone.

"When," she asked frantically.

"Just about ten minutes ago," I answered. Nobody can describe the wail of a parent learning their child is now dead. Now, I'm listening to it for the first time. Once she came back on the line I told her I'll wait for them to come to the hospital. In the meantime, she will call Lucien and I will contact the rest of the family.

I next tried to call my father. Nobody answered the phone and I did not want to leave such a message on his recorder. I then called my brother telling him what happened. He would contact my father at work to give him the bad news.

The rest of the time I spent in the conference room with Rev. Lewis and one of the social workers. It was rather ironic none of the social workers we were dealing with in the past was there. I could hear people talk around me, but I could not hear what they were saying. This went on until Eileen and her parents made it to the conference room. The four of us went into Pam's covered room. The trach and all the monitors she was hooked up to had been removed. She just lay there with her eyes closed appearing to be at peace with herself.

CPSIA information can be obtained at www.ICGtesting.com
Printed in the USA
LVOW06s0056280214

375394LV00005B/20/P